STAND AND DELIVER

A master of the art of public speaking reveals his techniques for success.

STAND AND DELIVER

A Handbook for Speakers, Chairmen
and Committee Members

by

Kenneth P. Brown

THORSONS PUBLISHERS LIMITED
Wellingborough, Northamptonshire

First published 1983

British Library Cataloguing in Publication Data

Brown, Kenneth P.
  Stand and deliver.
  1. Public speaking
  I. Title
  805.5'1   PN4121

ISBN 0-7225-0813-1

Printed in Great Britain by
Richard Clay (The Chaucer Press) Ltd,
Bungay, Suffolk

Acknowledgements

The author wishes to record his grateful thanks to the many kind friends whose advice and help have assisted in putting this work together.

In particular Mr N. J. LeGrice, Chairman of the Council of the Vegetarian Society for his expert advice in respect of Chairman's duties and points of procedure.

Four students qualify for 'Oscars':

Audrey whose maiden speech (on Womens Lib.) caused a tidal wave in the Lake District.

John who had the cool nerve to give MY lecture to a large audience just after taking my Course and a second 'Oscar' for getting away with it.

Jill who survived shipwreck on her maiden voyage (see 'On the Day).

Chris who asked the 64,000 dollar question after hearing my address on Chairmanship, etc. thereby causing me to consult no fewer than three experienced chairmen before giving my final complete reply. The exercise set at the end of this book is based on it.

(Students' full names are omitted to save any possible embarrassment. All my students helped me in one way or another. I thank them all.)

Contents

Preface

Following several successful years of conducting courses in public speaking and related subjects, this book was written in response to very many requests from those interested who have not been free to attend courses when or where held.

During the course of its writing my attention was drawn to a quotation of unknown origin but has been attributed to an army instructor. As it is a very neat summary of the construction of a lecture, I give it here:

'First I tells 'em what I'm going to tell 'em, then I tells 'em, then I tells 'em what I've told 'em.'

It should be noted that I have always asked pupils to practise on their own pet subjects as only thus could good results be expected. I therefore make no apology for the selected examples in this book being on *my* pet subject, but hasten to assure readers that that is the only reason and they are not intended in any way for propaganda purposes but solely as useful illustrations of structure.

I have done my best to help my readers to be more effective in their deliveries or better able to exercise control as the case may be, but I cannot provide the captive audience for the reader to practise on, and can only suggest that friends be persuaded to help in this respect.

The contents of their speeches are no concern of mine — the delivery is. This book, like the courses that have led up to it, is most suited to assist in giving talks of general interest or of a propaganda nature rather than the technical lecture which is the province of the more experienced speaker whose concern in any case is to convey knowledge rather than to inspire to action, and who would be perfectly justified in making far more reference to notes than I encourage among my students. Nevertheless there may be a few experts in their own field who find difficulty in conveying their fund of knowledge to others and may derive some benefit from the hints therein.

I was asked in my very first course whether sincerity was not far more important than oration. Then and now my reply is that sincerity is essential. To be effective a speaker must believe what he or she has to say, but the fact remains that there are very many sincere people who have difficulty in getting their message across. It is them for whom this book is written.

Finally my message to those who have never spoken to an audience and are fairly sure of their inability to do so — they 'shall inherit the Earth'. My star successes have been total novices.

1. Silence . . .

2. . . . Is Golden

Did you skip Chapter 1? You did! Then please go back and study it for at least a quarter of a minute. I will wait for you here.

Are you back? Good. You have now done the first exercise. Replying to your unspoken question, no, I am not a raving idiot. Chapter 1 represents the total silence that MUST precede every speech you make henceforth for the rest of your life.

How many times have you been able to hear every line of a play except the first one? Was it not drowned in the rustle of programmes and chocolate boxes, the coughs, shufflings and private conversations of the audience? Yet trained professional actors and directors seem to remain blissfully unaware that opening lines are all too often fed to stone deaf ears.

This warning will be repeated at intervals in this book and I make no apology for the repetition. At the start of any lecture I wait until the whole audience is gaping in silence and wondering if I have lost my notes or forgotten why I am there. From that moment on I can rely upon having their undivided attention. Their curiosity at its height, they hang on the opening words, wondering how I will fill the vacuum I have created. This is the moment of truth. A tame or hackeyed first sentence would be disaster. It should be strong, enigmatical, controversial or amusing according to the lecture to follow. More on this anon, but I would like to tell you an opening

I have used with effect in most of the courses I have conducted. After the long pause and the formal 'Mr Chairman, Ladies and Gentlemen' I pause again for a moment and then say 'You are now three quarters of the way through the course — but don't make for the door yet — we still have quite a lot of work to do.' The point in my opening remark is this. The hard part of giving a lecture is the preparation while the delivery is the last and easy quarter so when you find yourself on the platform and about to speak, if you have done your homework properly, you are at least three quarters through.

Sometimes I take a fiendish delight in keeping the audience waiting for any explanation at all until I have recounted an anecdote which I always slip in somewhere, telling the tale something like this . . . 'Before continuing I will give you an extract from one of the Sherlock Holmes stories which may at first seem to have no connection with the business in hand but you will find that actually it has. If it seems a little corny I will remind you that the plot has been used so many times that we are apt to forget that it was far from being a chestnut when first told by Sir Arthur Conan Doyle. It comes from "Silver Blaze" which is the story of a stolen racehorse of that name. Holmes and the faithful Dr Watson are returning by train from their investigations at the stables and Holmes is in a brown study. Curiosity and boredom eventually overcome Dr Watson who remarks "You seem to be very deep in thought Holmes. What is troubling you?" Says Holmes, "I am concerned with the remarkable incident of the dogs." "But the dogs did nothing" said Watson. "Quite so" said Holmes, "that was the remarkable incident".'

The reason for the inclusion of this anecdote in the course, as I then explain, is that the silence of the dogs at the time of the crime is a classic example of the power and eloquence of silence. Not only must all talks have an opening silence but pauses at convenient points throughout. This is one of the hardest but most important rules of good oratory.

None of the rules will save you if you have not prepared a good lecture beforehand, so a few chapters will later be devoted to the construction and we shall work slowly back to the platform fully armed to do battle but probably finding it will then be a 'push over'.

3. The Shorter Speech

i. Presentations

After long service it is usual for firms or other organizations to make a gift to an employee on retirement. This may be provided by the executive, the staff, or both. If from the staff then any one may get asked to make a suitable speech.

This is not at all a difficult assignment, the main ingredients being a reference to long and devoted service, with any special achievements given special mention. A few kind words about comradeship and how much the retiring employee will be missed should be followed by wishes for a long and happy well-earned freedom to pursue his own interests as and when he pleases.

Conclude with an expressed hope that he will keep in touch with 'The Old Firm' who will welcome news from him at any time.

If, on the other hand, the presentation is an award or diploma in respect of some specific achievement it becomes even simpler. Just make sure you have the details right and give suitable congratulations.

Presentations are not occasions for being funny. They are important to the recipient who may have worked very hard for the award. Any remark in the 'Aren't you lucky' class would be a calculated insult. And never be funny about retirement either as some people dread it.

ii. Votes of Thanks

No hard rules can be given under this heading as the service meriting the compliment is variable. The most usual is in respect of an address that has been delivered gratuitously by an outside speaker.

A suitable opening in such a case would be 'It is my pleasant duty to express, on behalf of all present, our appreciation of Mr/Mrs Blank for being so kind as to come and address us.' This may well be followed by something complimentary relating to content and quality of the address, but this can actually be quite difficult when in fact that quality was conspicuously lacking.

If the address was well prepared and delivered you have no problem, describing it as informative, encouraging, stimulating or whatever may be most appropriate to the case. Reference to something particularly significant or novel which had been included could add a note of sincerity to your words.

The real difficulty arises when the speech was delivered badly or inaudibly, or worse still when the content had been pointless or unacceptable. In such cases do avoid the standard escape routes which are unconvincing to the point of embarrassment to the guest speaker. I refer to saying that the speech was 'Interesting' or 'Has given us much food for thought' and, the crowning insult, 'It was very good of Mr Blank to come so far to address us.' That is all right as a supplementary compliment, but in isolation amounts to 'damned by feint praise'.

Then what is there left to say? Well, a bad speech is usually accompanied by copious notes, so try this one — 'We do appreciate what a great deal of work Mr Blank has put into preparing his address and feel we should record our gratitude. I therefore ask you to join me in a vote of thanks.' Then sit down and the audience will no doubt respond by clapping. Crisis over.

On the other hand you may have sat through an ill-prepared long-winded diatribe with no notes at all. These are usually very repetitive and rich in irrelevant anecdotes. The only convincing compliment you can deliver is 'How can we help but admire a speaker who can deliver so comprehensive an address entirely without notes.' He will probably never see through that one.

One last word. Get the speaker's name right! Lest you think I joke

I do in fact give you this as a serious warning — based on my own experience. Thanks were once given to 'Mr Jones' for an address of my own. The perpetrator was very nervous and I of course ignored it completely, but a celebrity might well be offended by such an error.

iii. Introductions

You may often find yourself having to introduce a speaker, performer, or perhaps a cine-projector operator, especially at a gathering on your own premises where it will be your duty as host to fulfil this function.

It is very easy, but nevertheless a few notes in hand are to be recommended. You must get the name right and, if in doubt, find out in advance how the speaker likes to be introduced. Some like to be 'Tom' to everybody for example, while others expect to have the full name announced. If there is a title, Sir, Lord, The Reverend, etc., then give it unless you have been asked not so to do.

Secondly, state fully and precisely what the person concerned has come to do and at whose invitation. On no account start with 'The speaker needs no introduction'. Not only is it hackneyed but is usually not true. A typical introduction might sound like this:

(Stand up, pause, and speak loud and clear.)

'Your attention please. It is my pleasure to introduce Mr John Blank who is here by invitation of our committee to address us on Bee-keeping on which subject he is a recognized authority. He has kindly consented to speak to us and, time permitting, will be pleased to answer any questions you may care to ask him afterwards. Will you please give a warm welcome to Mr John Blank' (at which point you indicate the speaker with a gesture, he will rise and you will take your seat).

iv. Toasts

We are not concerned here with long speeches after a dinner by the guest of honour for example. This might be a lengthy discourse ending up with a toast to the host society and for guidance on this see Chapter 4.

Toasts at parties or weddings are the more welcome for being spontaneous, witty and brief. The less conventional the better. You are on very safe ground if you ask all present to join you in wishes for many happy days ahead for the couple or person concerned, then raise your glass and repeat the name(s) and all will join in. The inclusion of a funny story is not advisable unless it is short, non-controversial and in good taste. If in doubt — don't.

Should you be presiding at a dinner you will normally be expected to open with the Loyal Toast which should be the first toast of the evening. Correct drill is to stand up and say 'Ladies and gentlemen, I will now ask you to rise and join me in the Loyal Toast.' When all are standing, lift your glass and say 'The Queen.' Do not say anything else. It is not to be coupled with anything else at all. I have recently heard a bit of subtle political propaganda slipped in with it. No one approved, nor did they repeat the extra bit with their toasts.

Any one other than the president on standing up to propose a toast should open with 'Mr (or Madam) President, distinguished guests (if any), ladies and gentlemen.' Then make any tribute, praise or whatever you wish to give before you actually ask the assembly to rise and give the toast. You may have been asked to do the honours in favour of some entertainers or the caterers, or perhaps absent friends. If you have not had a prior request to do so you will be on very dangerous ground to act spontaneously. It may have been pre-arranged for another to do it. Should you wish to include a short speech you must get it in before the actual toast. If you do not, at least half of those present will be on their feet and your words will be drowned in the responses. A little obvious perhaps, but if it is your first attempt you could get the cart before the horse.

v. Impromptu Speeches
You may be asked at very short notice to speak 'off the cuff' to a gathering for a variety of reasons, more particularly in place of an absent speaker or to fill in time until a delayed speaker makes an appearance.

Unless you are exceptionally well informed on the intended speaker's subject you will be well advised to steer clear of it. The speaker may turn up late and give an address that contradicts many of your own earlier observations. Or, even worse, he may say exactly what you said and you will have stolen his thunder in advance. Tell your audience that you have been prevailed upon at short notice to fill in, then that you have no intention to presume in any way to cover what the speaker will, it is hoped, in due course deal with more adequately himself. Then tell them what you do propose to talk about. It can be a related topic but better something quite different altogether than a pale shadow of what they have come to hear. You are safer on travel stories or amusing anecdotes of general interest to any audiences than to 'step in where angels fear to tread.' An audience is always sympathetic with anyone in your predicament, even if very disappointed at having to wait for the advertised address. Another reason for being asked at short notice to say a few words may be the opening of a bazaar or the introduction of some amateur entertainment.

Just make sure that you are clearly briefed on names and details and then jolly it through lightheartedly. Don't panic. The show will go on even if you do fluff your lines and sometimes slip-ups raise a laugh and lighten the tension for others more nervous than yourself. As soon as you have acquired a reputation as a speaker you may expect to be pushed on to numerous platforms at very short notice. I could give many examples but the prize one in my collection happened to me in York when I was asked, without any notice whatever to compere a fashion show in a big hall with television laid on. And there was half an hour's technical hitch before the cameras got going. I had to keep the large audience happy until it started to work so I just told them what had happened (or hadn't) and suggested they talked to each other until the wires were sorted out. At intervals I gave them progress reports (pure guesswork) and thanked them for being so patient, assuring them they would be well rewarded with the show lined up for them. It seemed to work. No one walked out.

Reverting to the much simpler matter of opening a bazaar, just remember that few will listen and in the hubbub fewer will hear. Tell them you hope and trust they will all have a jolly time and that as you feel sure they would rather do so, you will delay their pleasure no longer, adding 'I therefore have much pleasure to declare this bazaar open.'

4. The Longer Speech

i. Genesis

Invitations to give talks or lectures are usually made a few weeks in advance and if they are not, then any short-comings will be the fault of the organizers. Nevertheless the methods of preparation which follow may enable you to get something reasonably good together even in a short time.

You may be given a free hand to choose your own subject but if the theme is suggested to you and it is not consistent with your views or is beyond your capabilities even allowing time for research, then it is better to ask for an alternative or refuse altogether. Let us continue therefore on the assumption that the subject is 'up your street' and that you have time in hand to think up some appropriate material.

First think in general terms of the sort of audience you expect to have. The nature of the organization that has invited you will give you some idea and your theme will have to be put over in rather different terms to, say, an elderly ladies' club or a Rotary Club, or again a political group. Keep the picture of your audience in front of you.

Individuals have their inspirations at very different times and places, so rigid rules on getting started would only defeat the object. It is suggested however that you are never without a note book so that at any time you can jot down an idea, a phrase or any relevant memo that comes to you and may be forgotten. Some may prefer to sit down and do it all in one concentrated effort. Do what suits you best. In any case what you write down will almost certainly be a totally unreadable jumble of jottings in no logical order so the next job is to write it all out in some sort of sequence, 'licking it into shape' as it were.

Now read it straight through. You will find two things stand out. One is that it lasted five minutes and the other it makes plenty of sense to you but to a person uninitiated in the subject it will probably convey very little.

For a second attempt rewrite with supporting facts, figures and explanations as may seem desirable to give the whole picture to the least informed of your anticipated audience. All this could involve a lot of writing or typing but the very act of doing it is going to make it very much easier to remember when the time comes. However, I am often asked if it is permissible to use a tape recorder. There is no objection to this throughout the interim stages, and in fact it is most helpful to hear how it sounds, but you must type out the final finished lecture for reasons which later become apparent. In the absence of such a machine it can be handwritten but carbon copies will be needed and a large triplicate book will be almost essential. Type in double or even triple spacing and then you will be able to put in afterthoughts in their proper context without too many arrows, asterisks and marginal notes which cause much confusion. Carbon copies are not essential until the final typing as described in a subsequent chapter.

ii. The Long and Short of It

Tame titles and empty seats go together so unless you want a guaranteed flop before you have even started you are advised to think of a provocative or topical title to attract public interest. They cannot be expected to attend at a small hall to hear an unknown speaker unless their curiosity has been aroused. The audience will be limited to the committee and the more loyal members, all of them being already converted. So remember that goods sell on their names in the first instance. I once devised a title sufficiently provocative to fill any hall, namely, 'Those Vegetarians — Madmen or Missionaries?' The Committee of the Society who had invited me to give a talk of my own choosing vetoed the title and informed me by post that they were advertising the lecture as 'The History of Vegetarianism'. This tame alternative, apart from being useless for attracting an audience, had no connection with the proposed address which was already fully prepared. Also I was not competent to expound the history of the movement.

I exploded. The original title was reinstated, duly advertised, and on the night the hall was packed.

My advice, therefore, must be to think of a good title and resist all attempts to sabotage it. A last word before we pass on to the next stage. Will you please ask yourself why this book is divided into chapters. Why is any book so divided? Come to think of it, why is every book arranged likewise? If the theme or story is continuous why split it up?

The answer is that it makes it altogether more readable. We must have breaks, moments of relaxation, and the author knows best the points at which continuity is least interrupted by stopping for breath. Precisely the same applies to lectures, even short ones. Chapters do not need to be all of the same length but a lecture must be divided clearly into a convenient number of sections, each dealing with a different aspect of the subject.

I have already said in the Introduction to 'The Longer Speech' that every speech should open with a significant line. The same applies to a lesser degree with each section so you must make a brief pause between 'chapters' and re-open with a clear indication that you are breaking new ground and thus re-arouse interest. All sections should finish with some sort of conclusion and not just frizzle out. If it is a propaganda talk you are giving then the last line of the whole address should be epigrammatical, that is, the message in a nutshell. A tame finish undoes all your good work. Your audience should go home with your last words buzzing in their ears. Now to the next step. Having chosen your main title you should give each section of the talk a sub-title. These will be entirely for your own reference and not for announcement. Now see that the several sections are arranged in a logical order, the one tending to lead to the next with the last being the most important. As you will be re-typing it all do not hesitate to take a pair of scissors and shuffle the sections around bodily. You should soon be ready for the final typing in triplicate of the finished lecture but be sure to read the whole of it at just the speed at which you intend to deliver it, and thereby satisfy yourself that its length and content are just as you want them to be. A few minutes either way from the original target are not important but if it appears to be necessary to shorten it try cutting out nearly all the adjectives. You will find you have added to the strength. The over-use of superlatives has long ago stripped them of their force. 'Absolutely marvellous' now means precisely nothing.

On the other hand, should you need to lengthen the discourse you should endeavour to put in some more useful explanatory matter, supporting anecdotes or fresh material — NOT repetitions or any other kind of padding. Anecdotes are permissible if relevant and may be humorous if you are capable of raising a laugh. Some can tell jokes and some cannot. A talk which drags only bores so it is better to leave it short and fill in time on answering questions or in the final summing up rather than dilute it and destroy its punch. *The audience may emit yawns but it is the speaker who makes them.* Write that on the cover of your note book. Now go through the whole manuscript with a red pen and *underline all opening and closing sentences and any special key phrases* you are particularly keen not to omit whatver else you may forget. Be selective. Underlining is akin to emphasis. If you emphasize everything you emphasize nothing so do not let your underlining run away with you and merge into a continuous line.

The final typing in triplicate may now be done. The sub-titles need not be included unless you wish, but should appear for your own reference on the abbreviated notes that you will carry on to the platform.

The Card

Prepare in bold type, well spaced, on a single small sheet of paper or, better still, on a card the title of the speech, all sub-titles, and all the words, phrases and sentences you have underlined. You can even write these key lines with a poster pen on a large card or a number of cards which can be flicked over as the lecture proceeds. I recommend this latter method and usually punch holes in the cards, hold them together with a couple of treasury tags and add a blank card at the back which I bend double so that the whole contraption stands up at a convenient angle to be read at several paces. The punch holes should of course be at the bottom of each card and, if you wish, the tops can be cut to form tabs in different positions from end to end to avoid the risk of turning two cards over together (if you do you can rarely go back).

These brief and readily readable notes are almost essential and will be referred to many times in this book. To save enumerating the diverse forms that they may take to suit the convenience of the individual they will be called 'The Card' in every case.

Now try to give the talk to an imaginary audience using only the Card for reference. After all that typing you will find you remember far more than you had dared to hope. Well, after all you wrote it! You must know what is in it. And the card will (literally) keep you in order. If you can persuade one or more kind friends to be your audience it will be doubly beneficial as it will not merely be good practise but is actually a more severe test than the ultimate public delivery. The smaller the audience, and the more personal it is, the harder it is. Friends and relatives make you self-conscious — you wonder what they are thinking and a snigger or grin can throw you. It is quite impossible to imagine the reactions of ten million listeners or viewers so broadcasting is just a piece of cake. This is not just my own experience but one that has been confirmed to me by many, including novices.

iii. On the Day

The day arrives. Set out in good time and suitably dressed according to the formality of the occasion as far as you are able to judge. Better slightly too formal than risk insulting your audience by being over casual.

Check that you have with you any visual aids that you will need in support of your address, as for example a specimen of a product to which you intend to refer or a diagram you hope to pin to a blackboard. Do they have a blackboard on the premises? Is it in the room in which you will be speaking? Did you find out in advance? What a pity! Well if you are early enough you may get that sorted out but do not count on it.

By the way, they won't have any chalk and they won't have any drawing pins so take your own.

Of course take your notes and take some spare copies, but leave one safely at home so that your words of wisdom will not be lost for ever if you have to part with all the other copies.

Above all take the card.

On arrival contact the organizer and check the timetable as to starting time, interval, refreshments if any, question time and so on. If it has all been detailed to you in advance (unusual) it is as well to see that it is as planned.

Try to persuade the organizer as tactfully as possible to make all domestic announcements before your lecture. At worst settle for the interval. At least you can undo the damage in your summing up afterwards. What damage? Only wrecking the whole occasion from your point of view. You *must* have the last word. This is so important psychologically that it will be fully explained further on. Nothing should follow your final summing up other than a possible vote of thanks, which no one listens to anyway, and the Chairman announcing closure.

But how does a new speaker achieve this when it is a privilege to be asked to speak to some respected and established association? Well, try this 'Would you be so kind, in your own interests, to make your announcements at the beginning because I may get carried away and talk too long or drive some of your members home.' If they demur just add that it will help you too as it will give you a few more minutes to run through your notes. Of course you do not persist if they have set rules and are insistent and you will just have to put all the punch you can into your summing up so that its significance transcends and outlasts the secretarial patter about births, deaths, marriages, etc. in their ranks and the increase in the tea charges as from next month.

Hand one copy of the full notes of your talk to the organizer. This will prove very acceptable because, if you do not, one of two things will happen. Either some one, usually the Secretary, will have to take notes all the way through for their own records or to send to the local Press, or you will be asked afterwards for a copy of your notes and if you have not allowed for this may heaven preserve you from what they send to the Press from memory. If you send it on it will miss the Press date.

The other copies are brought along optimistically in case reporters are in attendance. They will almost certainly leave half way through and miss what you most wanted aired, but if you give them full sets of notes in advance they can go forthwith. There is a very good chance that the whole lot will be printed or at least an accurate précis from a manuscript with the key points ready underlined. If you have time before the event to prepare a précis your chances are even better.

So that is all copies disposed of. How about one for yourself? Certainly not! You will put the card on the table. This will help you to remember it all far better than groping for the place and stopping to read out bits. That is quite useless. The only other things you should place upon the table are 1. Books or papers of reference on technical matters which it is essential to quote exactly. The places should be clearly marked to save fumbling. 2. A note book which may be handy in question time. 3. Visual aids as aforementioned, but these should be out of sight until needed as they distract. The same applies to blackboard diagrams. Put the board back to front until you want it or your audience will try to work out what the diagrams mean instead of giving you their undivided attention.

In fact there is a very great deal that you cannot count on. By a quite extraordinary coincidence I had a telephone call, just before starting to type this chapter, from a very new speaker who had an engagement to address a meeting only two days after taking a course the weekend previous. I was forced to admit that I had not given any warning to the students that however diligently they followed the instructions they would not necessarily get co-operation from the home team. In the instance brought to my notice an early arrival was rewarded only by a long wait in the cold outside the premises followed by an invitation to help unstack chairs, nothing having been organized at all. This was just the beginning. A completely inexperienced chairman eventually arrived, was given an inadequate briefing, sat down and proceeded to make a total hash of the introduction. Later when questions were invited from the audience the speaker had to take control as the chairman played no part.

This is the worst case I have ever heard of but I am most grateful for having been prompted to include this warning that there are some very incompetent organizers who throw a totally unfair burden on the speaker. The young lady who took this all in her stride on her first public appearance is deserving of unqualified admiration. Rudyard Kipling might well have put one more line in his well-known poem 'If'. 'If you can cope in the face of organized chaos . . .' The last time I witnessed a speaker having to take over the chairman's duties it went almost unnoticed even by the chairman in question but the speaker had a lifetime of public speaking behind him. The only advice one can give is to be brave and play it by ear.

'The best laid plans of mice and men . . .'

iv. The 'Off'
Just before the 'off' there remain a few simple precautions which I recommend to you on the strength of my own regrets on occasion when I either did not know or did not bother.

One is to see that the chairman is properly briefed to be able to introduce you. He wants to give you a good send off but with the best of intentions he may fail through lack of information. It is probably not his fault but that does not help you one little bit, so have ready on a piece of paper:

Your name exactly as you are usually known and like it to be given which may be in full or an abbreviation.

Where you come from and/or The Association you represent.

Special Qualifications if related to the subject matter. (This is not blowing your own trumpet. The audience is entitled to know and if the sole qualification is years of experience or intensive preparation that is worthy of mention.)

The Title of the Lecture.

The chairman will be grateful for this and although he may well put it into his own words at least it will avoid a setback at the very beginning. Lest you think that this is an exaggeration let me just give you one example. I had to address a group whose usual chairman had not shown up and a very young and inexperienced woman was pushed into the 'hot seat'. She announced me to the meeting in the following terms — 'This is Mr Brown and I don't know what he has come to talk about'. My only emotion was to feel sorry for her as she was terribly embarrassed but had I been less experienced I might well have felt much sorrier for myself. I never let it happen again.

When handing the information slip to the chairman is a good moment to tell him if you would like a signal when you are nearing your time limit. A pre-arranged signal is far less embarrassing to all than an overt hint to stop when you need five minutes to conclude satisfactorily or no signal at all, leading you to exceed your time and upset the programme.

The 'stage' may be anything from a high platform to the corner of a small room. Try to avoid going on to it until invited to do so.

A popular mistake is to stride on and take a seat with every chance that you will select either the secretary's or chairman's position. You will get moved around to the detriment of your image.

Correct drill is to follow the chairman when he goes on stage and then to take the seat indicated to you. You may then put your notes down in front of you (the card of course, not the full manuscript) so that you will not have to fumble in pocket or bag for them later. Of course there may not be a table in which case you will have to keep your card in your hand and any display items you have brought will have to be disposed of under the seat or on an adjacent empty one if you are lucky. When you reach the time to stand up you are advised not to move too far away from the table. Away out in front the novice will feel all alone in Siberia faced by ravenous wolves, but with a friendly table or chairback upon which to rest an occasional nervous hand for comfort one is in a castle surrounded by docile well fed pets — which is much nearer the truth than you might think as hostile audiences are rare in the extreme (I have yet to meet one) and in particular they are sympathetic towards new or nervous speakers.

The chairman has introduced you. You STAND UP. Take it calmly. The initial silence follows and lasts until the audience is also silent, ready and waiting. About a quarter of a minute is usually ample.

Now turn to the chairman and say 'Mr (or 'Madam') Chairman', then, turning to the audience, continue with 'Ladies and Gentlemen'. There are permisible variations where for instance the audience is all of one sex or where a special relationship exists, as for example you might say, when speaking on the home ground, 'Mr Chairman and fellow members'. Formalities can often be relaxed as the event continues but it must start with formal acknowledgement of The Chair.

The carefully packaged 'goods' can now be pushed smoothly over the counter, but a whole chapter will be devoted to the handling thereof to be sure of 'satisfied customers'.

But wait. If I try your patience it is in a good cause. First I must explain why the words 'STAND UP' are in bold type. It is quite essential to stand unless you are content to have the meeting degenerate into a cosy chat with all your homework wasted. It is sufficiently important in fact to merit half a chapter to itself before we go on safari into that fearsome jungle where actually the fiercest roar you will ever hear will be a snore from some old chap who comes in out of the rain and has no intention of listening in any case.

v. 'Standing Orders'

'Nobody's head must be higher than the King's'. Those words are spoken by the King himself in the very well-known musical 'The King and I' in the scene where he is (literally) laid low by illness and the children's governess is standing over him to address him. She is commanded by the King for the sake of his prestige to grovel on the floor, he being unable to rise.

Pompous? Granted, but nevertheless of the greatest significance to us. There *is* a link between relative head levels and authority and one does not have to go as far back in history as the period of this play, nor does one have to travel abroad, to find a monarch whose shorter stature than his queen's must have made life hell on earth for photographers who, either out of respect or by reason of official promptings, used all angles and every trick in the book so that in all published pictures of their majesties together the above Siamese protocol would appear to have been observed.

Let us leave the Court and return to the lecture room. The standing speaker sees all the audience and can be seen by them, even the back row being able to follow every word and gesture. That is not, however, the main reason why it is so important to stand, for the lowest of platforms will adjust any question of levels. It is a psychological matter. If you put yourself at the same physical level as your listeners by being seated as they are your audience will accept this declaration of equality, albeit subconsciously, and will not hesitate to join in. So your carefully prepared and rehearsed discourse may develop into a multilateral discussion, richer in red herrings than Billingsgate Market, and sidetracked out of all recognition.

Before somebody writes to tell me of an exception to the 'standing' rule I think I will forestall the attack. When an employee is 'on the carpet' the employer is seated and the victim standing. Quite so. Privilege in an office is vested in desks, carpets and comforts, a tradition that dies very hard. I could tell so many stories about this it is perhaps better to leave the bureaucrats to run their own kingdoms undisturbed and get on with the business in hand.

Let it not be thought that I expect any lecturer to seek power over audiences or to exult therein. The sole aim is to gain silent attention and establish a mutual respect.

I have referred above to the audience being in a position not only to hear you but to see your gestures. A word of warning on this point before we pass on. Gestures should be very well controlled as they are in the same category as emphasis; that is to say, if you wave your arms about and thump the table nearly all the time it levels out and loses all significance. Unless it is totally unexpected it has little point and is so often a refuge of ineffective speakers it is always suspect. The less the better, but nevertheless it must be allowed that it is a legitimate mode of expression and can be an aid to both speaker and audience in making a point and may relieve tension on the one hand and sustain interest on the other.

A non-stop windmill, however, serves only to tire and irritate. Do not be misled by the perpetual gesticulations of the French whose mode of speech does not permit selective emphasis.

Now, the all-important question of reading whole or part of your address. Don't! It is even worse than sitting down to speak. Reading out a few quotations is all right, especially as it is vitally important for them to be accurate, and the same applies to statistics and technical passages. These should be to hand and marked so that groping is avoided, but continuous reading is out. No matter how well it is done the whole impact is weakened and the very act of looking downward has all the effects described in connection with sitting down to speak.

Would you like to know what your audience is thinking while you read to them? They are wishing they had been provided with copies so that they could have read them at home in comfort without missing a good dinner and their favourite TV show. They are speculating on the chances of catching a bus home instead of sitting on a hard seat any longer with the risk of a walk home in the rain.

With your eyes on the audience you can assess their reactions and respond to them. You are selling your personality as much as the subject. Wrap yourself up in paper and you project little and sell nothing.

You should in fact keep in touch with all your audience by turning this way and that, not forgetting the back of the room. Obvious? Perhaps, but it is all too easy to stare fixedly ahead, a fault against which I have continually had to fight.

A word is necessary here concerning speaking to a 'mike'. Amplifier systems are in ever increasing use and one must be prepared for this. By turning the head too far from the microphone words, and even whole sentences, may be lost to the listeners. Look around occasionally but pause while doing so.

This restriction will, however, depend to some extent on the quality of the equipment in use, and you will do well to arrive early and try to get an opportunity to test the instrument in advance, not forgetting the volume. Ask some one to sit at the back of the room and tell you how it comes over. *Do not shout*. That would be 'keeping a dog and barking yourself.'

Should you be privileged to speak on television or radio there is no need to worry at all. They will look after you and the volume. You can turn your head considerably without loss of sound, and, as I know to my cost, even a whisper comes across clearly. In the course of a broadcast I once whispered an aside to the chairman which went out loud and clear to some millions of listeners.

But we are primarily concerned with more general occasions than broadcasting, especially beginners who will not expect to speak under such conditions until more experienced.

As though my advice not to look away from the microphone needed proof a perfect example has just been brought to my notice in the course of writing this chapter. A recent week-end conference which some of my friends attended was successful except for one tedious and wasted hour when a well-informed speaker completely failed to come across by reason of mumbling, fidgetting, and turning his head away so often, that the audience could not follow him at all. Calls to him to speak up fell on deaf ears, and I must add that quite clearly the chairman did not do his job.

At the other extreme I should like to tell you of a holiday incident on a coach trip in Cornwall. The driver gave a running commentary on places of interest *en route* through an amplifier system which he rendered superfluous by shouting straight into the mike all the time, thereby blasting our ear drums and failing completely to achieve his purpose. On reaching Lands End I decided I could not stand a repetition on the return journey by another route, so for his sake as well as the passengers I risked my neck by telling the driver very politely how to use a 'mike'.

He agreed, rather reluctantly, to experiment, but as another passenger stayed on the coach to back me up he gave in.

After persuading the driver to speak quietly we heard every word clearly and left him completely convinced, with the result that the second half of our trip was enjoyed by all.

Projectors

This chapter would not be complete without some reference to the use of projectors and slides to accompany talks, with or without microphones, though one may question that this item might be more appropriately placed under 'Triumphs and Disasters'.

It is essential to have the apparatus positioned and tested in good time before the event. Long delays are commonplace as are slides showing out of order or upside down. The step from the sublime to the ridiculous may well be a slide.

Sometimes the speaker and operator are one but this is to be avoided if possible as the commentator is best placed beside the screen *facing the audience*, and as it may well be necessary to point out particular features on the screen *without stepping in front of it* a stick is desirable for the purpose. There are simple signalling devices for changing to the next picture.

Should the speaker be using a mike it is imperative to have a detached one held in the hand, or the voice will simply disappear every time it becomes necessary to turn the head screenwards.

Never turn your back on the audience — ask any schoolmaster!

But it may be necessary for the commentator to have notes, and as the room is presumably in almost total darkness one must have some light whereby to read them. It would appear that one needs to have four hands! Hand mike, pointer, notes and torch. That way lies chaos. An illuminated music stand would solve it quite easily, but is there one available and any sockets within reach to connect up? Remember to bring adaptors and spare flex.

vi. Some Expressions to be Avoided

So far we have considered only the nature of the content without reference to the structure or style. Before moving on to that, I feel that this is the moment to interpolate a few 'don'ts'.

We all have pet words and phrases which we use more than we know and they are likely to creep into our jottings. Irritating reiterations must be eliminated before we get anywhere near the finished speech. Two favourites are 'basic' and 'fundamental'. They are both perfectly good words to use but they should not recur in every other paragraph.

My next 'don't' is very important (I am tempted to say 'fundamental') and that is the everlasting 'I think' or 'In my opinion'. Will you please try to remember that the entire address is your opinion. The audience is there to hear what *you* think and the foregoing phrases are nothing but apologies, as though to say 'In *my* opinion but probably not any one else's.' The only time when such expressions are appropriate is when they are comparative, as for example 'George Bernard Shaw thinks . . . but in my opinion . . .'

While we are on the subject of apologetic words, a very popular one in speech or correspondence is 'surely' — a word used only by the unsure. Check yourself on this next time you find you are using the word. When I look at a page full of letters from readers in a newspaper I have no time to waste reading the silly ones so I glance first at each as I come to it and if it contains that word I pass on to the next letter. A few exceptions no doubt exist but on balance I save time and lose little benefit.

One of the worst apologetic phrases is 'you know'. It becomes a habit of which the perpetrator is unaware and was recently heard in every sentence spoken by a jockey being interviewed after a sensational win. He was the hero of the hour and yet was in effect apologizing for everything he said. Had the interviewer in fact known it all then the whole interview would seem to have been entirely unnecessary. Similarly, if a lecturer assures his audience that they already know it all then his address, by his own reckoning, is a total waste of time.

Repetitive pointless words or phrases can be very irritating but they are curable. A tape recorder can be very helpful if self observation should prove inadequate. Few of us know our own bad habits until we hear them played back to us. 'Er' and 'um' are quite the most usual. In a fifteen minute test maiden speech one of my students included fifty-seven 'um's'. In his second attempt the number was down to about a dozen which is a remarkable accomplishment considering that to this day I still catch myself emitting that silly syllable in unguarded moments.

Another silly irritant is 'You know what I mean' but this one is usually perpetrated in conversation rather than in speeches, as is the meaningless opening of 'anyway' to nearly every sentence.

Why do any of us do it? It is reluctance to leave even a split second blank. We see moments of silence as our enemies and only as confidence grows with experience do we recognize them as our friends.

And now my pet hate. 'At this point in time' (or sometimes '. . . this moment.'.) is a current favourite expression having *now* reached epidemic proportions. What is wrong with the simple word 'Now'? Why five words to replace one? I suspect it is done for dramatic effect and came to us from across the Atlantic, but its ceaseless reiteration has long since destroyed its impact and a decent burial is overdue.

On completion of a Speakers' Course which I had conducted, the editor of a journal sent me a proof of an interview he had with me and he quoted me as having used the above five-word phrase when in fact I had, in the Course, told my pupils always to avoid it. I got that editor out of bed at midnight to stop it going to press until corrected.

Though I claim no qualifications to entitle me to give my readers a grammar lesson, I think I may be pardoned for drawing attention to a few very common errors perpetrated not only on many platforms but by no means rare in broadcasts. There may be others but I will content myself with the following examples:

1. Never say '*Very* unique' or '*Very* nominal'. Both words are absolute and make the comparative adjective quite out of place.
2. 'Infer' and 'Imply' are freely interchanged despite their opposite meanings. To imply is to *convey* a message — to infer is to *deduce* therefrom. The expression, therefore, 'What are you inferring?' means 'What are you deducing from my remarks.'
3. The third howler in my list can be quite unintentionally funny. It all hangs on the suffix 'ing', and usually rears its treacherous head in the word 'being'. For example, what is wrong with this? 'Being a wet day I went and sat in a shelter.' Nothing — except that you have called yourself a 'wet day'! No doubt you can think up funnier ones. Harmless indeed, but if you think I make heavy weather over a quibble I can assure you it is very worrying to attract sniggers in a serious discourse and not to know why. To avoid this particular example you have only to put 'it' before 'being' or rearrange the sentence to read 'As it was a wet day I went . . .'
4. Nearly everyone, including TV interviewers, perpetrate this one, but that does not make it right. It is the simple difference between singular and plural which mix no better than oil and water. I refer

to 'Those sort (alternatively 'Those kind' or 'type'). It must be 'This' or 'That' sort because 'Sort' is collective and singular. '*Those sorts*' would be all right but though grammatically in order would seldom be intended.

5. The double past — a very common error. E.g. 'I would have liked to have had the opportunity.' This means that at some time in the past the speaker would have liked to have had (at an even earlier date) the opportunity. Correct forms are: 'I would like to have had . . .' or 'I would have liked to have . . .', i.e. one past only.

vii. Triumphs and Disasters

If you have never sat alongside a discourse and watched it go out to the audience you now have an opportunity. In the diagrams associated with this chapter the thick black line is the speech, progressing in time from left to right and varying up and down with the volume, power and effectiveness of the delivery.

Figure 1 depicts the least effective lecture in all the world, the dreariest, droning discourse that it is possible to inflict. May you never have to sit through one (I have) and a plague upon you if you ever perpetrate one after you have digested this chapter.

In this one, as soon as introduced, the speaker remains seated and buries his face in notes on the table so, as you see, it starts as near floor level as possible and seldom rises any higher as it progresses in a dreary monotone without a hint of a pause from one end to the other. It might not be inappropriate to call this type a prayer meeting as the whole congregation is indubitably so engaged but not so much by reason of inspiration as desperation.

Their prayers are destined to be answered eventually in a manner calculated to provide the only drama of the occasion. This timeless and untimed discourse grinds to a halt by petering out and dropping through the floor boards into oblivion (for who shall remember what was inaudible in the first place).

Then where is the drama? Well, you will note the order of

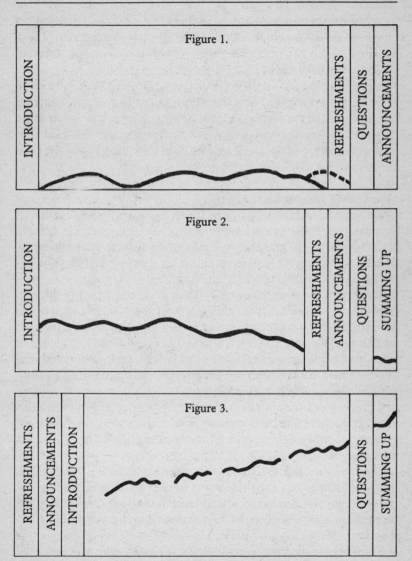

Figure 1.

INTRODUCTION

REFRESHMENTS

QUESTIONS

ANNOUNCEMENTS

Figure 2.

INTRODUCTION

REFRESHMENTS

ANNOUNCEMENTS

QUESTIONS

SUMMING UP

Figure 3.

REFRESHMENTS

ANNOUNCEMENTS

INTRODUCTION

QUESTIONS

SUMMING UP

programme thought up by the committee responsible for the event (It has to be a committee. One person could not have done it. It is said that the camel was to have been a horse but a committee designed it) so we find the saga of untimed and unpredictable length dying in one of two ways, either five minutes before the kitchen is ready for the next item (panic and impromtu padding from the chair) or like the story of the locusts in The Arabian Nights the talk was not intended ever to end and is finally mercifully drowned in a rattle of tea cups, the crunching of many biscuits and the happy release of bottled-up gossip reverberating round the room.

In due course an attempt is made to elicit questions from the re-assembled audience, such as have stayed, but any connection between these and the hidden wisdom reclining on the speaker's table will be purely coincidental. As the caretaker rattles an ominous key the Secretary rattles off the domestic announcements to the backs of the departing throng. Some of these may be remembered. Little else.

Figure 2 calls for little comment. It is a normal, average talk such as we have all heard many times. The speaker is standing up so at least the discourse started some six feet from the floor. It is what would be described in a report or vote of thanks as 'interesting', the word we fall back on when there is really nothing else to be said, and it does have undulations sufficient to retain the interest of those who really came to listen. It was prepared and timed so it ended bang on time to the delight of the organizers.

The programme would appear to have been arranged with some thought as the announcements are dealt with in the more domestic part of the proceedings and the chairman will now know just how long can be allowed for questions before the *summing up*. An experienced speaker, when asked if willing to answer questions will always stipulate that it will be subject to a few minutes being reserved to sum up. If he does not the questions and answers may have left the audience in a confused state of mind and a tidying up is very necessary. The summing up is, however, too often regarded by the speaker as an opportunity to sum up the questions. Not so.

In the next part of this chapter we will pursue that point. Before we move on please note that in *Figure 2.* there were no clear, distinct recognizable pauses from start to finish. That may be rather below average performance but if I seem to be harsh in my criticism I submit that it is quite the most common fault among speakers. It takes courage to pause but it is so very rewarding.

If you have not witnessed a performance by the Danish entertainer, Victor Borge, I beg you to endeavour to do so. He appears on television from time to time in this country and holds his audiences spellbound for a solid hour almost entirely on his own. If you repeat his jokes to others afterwards you may fail to raise even a snigger for the simple reason that his humour is elementary in the extreme, almost childish, and to get any response must be retailed as he said it. And you cannot. That is why he is paid many thousands of pounds for every performance. The secret is perfect timing, long pauses and the unexpected punch line coming like a flash of light in a dark room.

Why is it that Billy Graham can fill the Wembley Stadium with the same message employed by many a person to lull his dwindling congregation to sleep? The main difference is the timing. Billy Graham's calculated silences are the most eloquent pieces of nothing ever launched into the ether.

Figure 3 is the speakers dream. It is based on the assumption that the necessary strings have been tactfully pulled to get the programme in the right order with tea and twitter disposed of first, domestic trivia safely transmitted and the Chairman left with nothing to distract him from conducting the main business in uninterrupted sequence.

Now take a good look at the design. Does not this lecture in full flight look much more exciting than the previous two? After a dramatic pause it shoots straight up in the air and lifts the audience with it. Comparatively high spots recur at intervals and each section should end on a note of promise leading on to the next. Then you make them wait for it. Each section is of very similar construction but it is not expected that each will start on shock tactics on a par with the first. You reserve a trump card for last and the order of the several phases of the theme should ideally be arranged so that you can end up with a pretty powerful or cryptic last line. Never fade out.

If you have handled it well you should inspire some bright questions. One of my students taught me something which I consider well worth passing on, subject to one warning. He left something significant unsaid to give some questioner a chance to raise the matter and receive a prompt and full answer. The only risk is that it will not be asked, but all is not lost. The omitted item can be brought into the summing up afterwards so the opportunity is deferred but not lost.

It rests with the chairman to decide whose turn it is to ask a question and more will be said on this under chairmanship duties in the appropriate part of this book.

Meanwhile it should be mentioned here that 'questions' must not be statements unless unrestricted comment has been specifically invited. Chairmen should be on their guard against false questions designed to air a point of view, sometimes scarcely related to the subject of the lecture. They usually begin 'Does the speaker agree that . . .?' and be ruled out of order unless the connection with the address becomes readily apparent and the speaker is willing to reply.

When the chairman decides it is time to stop questions, and discussion if allowed, he will invite you to sum up. If he does not you are recommended to ask his permission to do so as it really is important that the meeting should not terminate on the confusion of question and answer.

The best time to make sure of being allowed the privilege of the last word is the point where the chairman asks you if you are willing to answer questions (this may be at the outset or after the talk). You should reply that you are quite willing, subject to some time being reserved for your final summing up.

I repeat that this does not mean a rehash or analysis of the questions. It is your chance to bring the meeting back to the original topic from which it will almost certainly have shot off at a tangent several times unless a tough chairman has kept them on the subject.

Your summing up should be almost exactly what you have written on your card, or in other words a neat precis of your address in a very few words and finishing with what you consider to be the essential message you have come to convey. Observe that the last thick black line on *Figure 3* is almost climbing up the wall. You finish on what you want them to be talking about all the way home and right through breakfast the morning after.

The most successful of all revivalists, the most persuasive of all public speakers in the whole history of oratory must be Billy Graham, and it is fortunate for the world that his hypnotic influence was wielded in a good cause. His audiences sang 'Alleluia' all the way home on trains and buses from his great gatherings. This was achieved by masterly timing. What else? He preached nothing new.

viii. Examples

Example 1.
As a very straightforward first example I am selecting a fairly standard address that I have given frequently with only a few variations.

The subject is Vegetarianism in its many aspects, which leads itself ideally to division into convenient sections, each one leading on to the next to maintain continuity.

In preparation of any such address one would first jot down the main headings, consider the appropriate order thereof, and in this instance the result would appear something like this:

1. Health
2. Compassion
3. Inherited conviction
4. Religion
5. Economics

It is not necessary for me to give the address in full. The general pattern will suffice in this instance. Taking each heading:

1. Start with something provocative like this — 'First Class health comes from First Class food, and meat is second hand and therefore second class. Food from the soil is first hand.'
   You would then cite such evidence as you already knew or could find out. Then follow with — 'The desire for better health is the most usual initial motive for trying vegetarianism. It could fail if approached negatively, that is giving up meat but putting nothing of value in its place.'
   Now enumerate the basic protein foods recommended. Conclude the first section somewhat like this — 'Health is, however, by no means the sole consideration of adherents to the cult, and contacts made with other vegetarians soon elicit the many other motives.
   Now *pause*. That was the lead up to the next stage.

2. 'Having become aware that all the slaughter you had been led to accept as 'cruel necessity' was not a necessity at all, you will feel very guilty about having aided and abetted.
   The compassionate aspect will increasingly take over from the more selfish interest in your own health.'
   Follow with evidence of the alleged cruelties, avoiding overstatement which offends and is counter-productive.

   Continue:

   'Many join the Vegetarian movement by reason of compassion alone. However noble the motive the dangers must be watched. A balanced diet is necessary to maintain good health, and advice should be sought or health may suffer and the whole project be dropped.'
   (Give some basic advice and say where further guidance is available.)
   'A slow and lasting change is more beneficial than an emotional and zealous but short-lived experiment.'

3. 'Those born into vegetarian families are fortunate indeed, and today there are many of them, but they are the least enthusiastic as they have never known anything else. It is not an experimental change or a mission but just a fact.
    Recent converts are the most outspoken as in most causes. Happily there are some notable exceptions, the membership including third and fourth generation active supporters.'

4. 'The western world is predominantly carnivorous but a global census would reveal very different figures. Although climate and economics have their influence there are vast numbers who abstain from flesh food for purely religious reasons, Hindus and Buddhists being the majority.
    It is significant that great religious leaders and philosophers of a diversity of faiths have held and preached the view that vegetarianism is an aid to spiritual development.'

(Follow with examples, e.g. Plato, Buddha, Tolstoy, G. B. Shaw, John Wesley, General Booth.)

5. The world's biggest problem for the future is that of feeding an ever-increasing population on a decreasing available fertile acreage of land. The acres used for grazing and growing cattle food could feed six times as many people as does the meat produced, and the time must come when the world accepts vegetarianism or perishes. Those who are then prepared will have no difficulty in accepting the change and will be better off than the enforced reluctant converts.
    It is better to go than be pushed.

Platform Notes
After re-writing the above notes in full and underlining the key points, it is then necessary to prepare the very brief notes therefrom to be taken on to the platform. They should look something like this:

Opening — First class health cannot be expected from second-hand food.

1. Health — the most usual motive. Giving up meat but putting nothing in its place.

2. Compassion — 'Cruel necessity?' Not necessary, therefore only cruel.

3. Inherited — Life vegetarians lucky so to be — but much less enthusiastic.

4. Religion — Mainly oriental. N.B. Hindus and Buddhists. Leaders from Plato to General Booth (list if necessary).

5. Economics — Growing populations — Shrinking acres.

End — 'Go or be pushed'.

Example 2
The following address is given in full as it is a useful example of structure. It is on the same subject as the first example but, as opposed to being for beginners only, it was addressed also to many well informed members and attempted to satisfy both.

As it was well received and held the attention of the audience for about an hour, it may serve readers as a working model.

Those Vegetarians — Madmen or Missionaries?

There is a law. A law as old as every living species on the planet. The Law is 'Thou shalt not be different.' In the jungle it operates somewhat fiercely. In the other jungle we laughingly call civilization the application is subtler but nonetheless effective.

The existence of this law was brought to my notice when I visited one of my old schoolmasters in retirement some twenty years after leaving school. I gathered for the first time why it was that the headmaster had actively disliked me from first meeting. I was different.

But he little knew how much this simple analysis had explained. In the intervening years I had felt the force of this law and been guilty of applying it too. When I was younger and greener (I cannot say in my 'salad days' for they had not begun) I found myself plagued by zealots of the fleshless cult and my simple verdict was . . . MAD TO THE LAST MAN. Did they not know that the three corners of our island rested firmly on three stout pillars, the bible, the Union Jack and roast beef. Was it not sacrilege? Ping pong on the high altar?

Came the day when my digestion caught up with me. The traditional roast and stodge washed down with milky coffee were not merging harmoniously with a sedentary occupation so I cast an envious eye and turned a more willing ear to the erstwhile lunatic minority and put one tentative foot into their strange world of cold green lunches which kept them painlessly awake and warm all through each winter afternoon.

But it was still only a minor issue and strictly for lunch-time. I had another mission of my own. I was busy telling an unheeding England how to run its monetary system and thereby solve all its problems. But at least I learned something from the experience and that is that in any reform movement whatever you trip over vegetarians at every turn. Too many by far to be attributable to coincidence.

It was my very good fortune to meet Edgar Saxon, editor of a health paper, who gently pointed out to me that any scheme to give the people more money to spend was almost useless while they remained the prey of advertisers who led them to waste nearly all of it on devitalized and harmful foods.

I could hardly dispute this opinion. Saxon himself was a convincing advertisement for his beliefs and teachings. He radiated vitality. I was hooked . . . one of the mad minority. One of the martyrs and smugly proud of it.

Before we are tempted to get too smug let us examine our own reactions to the non-conformist. We who like to regard our own difference as enlightenment are no less intolerant of the extremist within our own ranks who dare to blur our precious image with their originality.

We are united in our respect for all life. We are divided on dietetic detail. And why not? There is plenty of room for individuality in a movement that stands for a way of life that is not built on a foundation of death nor one governed by spartan rules. You are forgiven if you think us a little mad sometimes but never accuse us of being dull.

On the main issue there can be no deviation. We accept the commandment 'Thou shalt not kill' and insist that it means just what it says. No more and no less. And this is least accepted where it is most reiterated.

Most of us agree that meat is harmful but our reasons for abstention are more humanitarian than self-defensive. Beyond that we are free to think and act as we like. The initiate reads all the right books and knows all the answers . . . only to find someone thriving on the opposite. Truly one man's meat is another man's poison. I will spare you my life story but an autobiographical note may bring some comfort to those who would join us willingly if they could bring their favourite vices with them. Why not? The worst that will happen to you is that you will attract the criticism of those who have read a different book and delight to predict your early doom. My own name is mud because I smoke a pipe without choking to death and drink enough black coffee to float a battleship. My survival is an affront to their pet beliefs.

New acquaintances assume that I live mainly on salads and fruit. I consume approximately two salads a year and fresh fruit is the only food that has ever put me in hospital.

We generally agree on the virtues of wholefoods as opposite to the depleted much advertised brands, especially in the case of bread . . . as white as the driven snow. Food and detergents get whiter every day the same as your hair does when the end is in sight. The Chinese seem to understand this and put on white for mourning. How right they are. White bread needs no jam. It jams up the whole system unaided. If you ever run out of blotting paper try white bread. It is quite effective and remarkably similar in texture and nutritional value. White sugar starts on your teeth and pursues its destructive path right through the system. The cube root of all evil.

Opinions are divided on milk but personally I gave up milk and catarrh together when I found that, like Juno's Swans, they are coupled and inseparable. You may continue to enjoy butter if you have no objections to rheumatism. Never let it be said that you have no free choice. I cannot suggest you take this all with a pinch of salt or the anti-salt section will set upon me.

But what a crashing bore if we agreed about everything. Vegetarianism should never be thought of in terms of renunciation because it is only at the very beginning that one is in the least conscious of this aspect. It is not negative. It is a very positive and comprehensive way of life that has to be experienced and cannot adequately be expressed in words.

It is very tempting at this point to pour out an emotional discourse on all the mental, physical and sometimes even spiritual benefits attainable through vegetarianism, but that is not my line so you will be spared any such sermon. It would in any case take a series of lectures and the whole lot would not be one half as effective as giving it a practical trial with a bit of guidance — available for the asking. I do not necessarily mean by way of books, nor do I mean only the benefit of advice our Society would willingly provide. I was once consulting an osteopath who also practised nature cure and was by way of being a philosopher. Philosophy was an unsolicited extra service administered free with the treatment. This particular oracle was trying to persuade me to read some book or other and I told him that I hated reading. He astonished me by agreeing that it was much overrated because whenever you really need to know something there will be somebody at your elbow to tell you. And this has proved to be true.

I have by no means finished with the law Thou shalt not be different. Why do all creatures in all ages seek to enforce this law? They do so because there is security in conformity. The first law of nature is the survival of the species and all change constitutes a threat and must be contained.

The human race instinctively rather than consciously wields the weapon of APATHY and only brings up the heavy artillery of ANTIPATHY when the stifling effects of the purely negative treatment have failed. Any missionary will tell you that apathy is the harder weapon to combat. How can you hit out at what is not there?

It will avail you nothing to rail against the public for their lack of interest in whatever cause you hold dear. Apathy is a built-in defence mechanism practised by us all and new ideas must have the force and persistence to break through or they have not stood up to the test and deserve to fail. And it was the frustrated leader of a revolutionary minority from whom I first heard that. In due course his movement died of apathy and to his credit he blamed himself and his doctrine — not the unheeding public.

Try to picture a community in which every new idea was readily adopted. The confusion which surrounds us today would be but a pale shadow of the consequent chaos.

So much for NEW ideas. The vegetarian philosophy is as old as time. It has had its adherents down the ages . . . leaders of men and whole peoples have followed them. Plato and Socrates for example. The pursuit of health and hygiene formed an integral part of many early beliefs and the ancient Greeks were quite a good advertisement for their regime.

A loftier motive was more evident with the advent of Buddha who preached a doctrine of physical purity as being essential to spiritual development. His followers may be counted in millions. Four hundred years later the early Christians appear to have had a very similar outlook. As to the case of Jesus Himself, it has been debated down the ages. We who have long found it difficult to accept the image of the Good Shepherd devouring His sheep, have welcomed the revelations of the Dead Sea Scrolls concerning the early training Jesus received among the Essines, a strictly vegetarian order. It would now appear that the logical answer has been the right one all along.

In more recent times there have been many more great thinkers and leaders whose teachings have encompassed a respect for all life and not exclusively for their own species.

John Wesley was one. To appeal to a different section of the community came General Booth to deliver much the same message in another tempo. His request to his officers to follow his vegetarian example fell on ears deafened by too many trumpets.

More successful mass followings incorporating vegetarianism have been those of the Hindus, the Jains and the Zoroastrians. It would seem to be the advanced(?) Western peoples who predominantly keep up the sacrificial rites of their primitive ancestors.

Other original and outspoken thinkers include the poet Shelley, the playwright George Bernard Shaw (always at least fifty years ahead of his generation), the esoteric religious writer Dr Anna Kingsford, and the man of so many parts, Count Leo Tolstoy.

We must not omit reference to Albert Schweitzer or the great living example, Krishnamurti who is not nearly so well known as he deserves to be. Personally I rate his teachings above all the rest but if you draw me out on that we shall have an all night sitting.

A little nearer to the earth are the leaders in their own particular spheres who have spread the message by example rather than by words. I am thinking of Dr Barbara Moore who did the John O'Groats to Lands End jaunt on a diet consisting almost entirely of dried fruit and nuts. She actually won an outright convert *en route*. A well known suet firm sponsored a rival marcher who had to give up but switched to Dr Moore's diet and finished the trip.

Then there is Bill Pickering, the channel swimmer and Dave Keeler the long distance cycling champion for years on end. There are many more and stars of stage and screen galore. I am told that Twiggy is the latest recruit but I am not sure if this is a boost to our vital statistics.

We certainly have not been without our missionaries, and if they be mad I would be proud to be incarcerated in the same institution.

Despite these encouraging examples the battle is not over yet. So we had better take stock of our ammunition. It will take a lot more than name-dropping to enlist the mass support that is needed to consolidate the great advances of recent years. The public attitude is more sympathetic than it has ever been. No longer are we in disgrace and as scared as a nudist of confessing our interests to employers, neighbours or friends.

Both apathy and contempt are on the run but how now shall we rally the extra support we need to finish the job and to end once and for all the horrors of the factory farm and the slaughter house?

Would that I could give you a simple answer but there isn't one. There are many. And the aspect that is of paramount importance to YOU may be of little significance to your neighbour. We could speak of taste or hygiene and health only to be asked 'What of the suffering of the animals? Should not your motive be less self-centred?' Or we could champion the cause of the beasts and be confronted with that time-honoured chestnut . . . 'Are you trying to starve my children to save the animals. Actually we keep a splendid stock of third and fourth generation vegetarians to laugh that one off and at the same time deftly dispose of the popular jibe that vegetarians lack virility.
Critics ask if we have any idea of the economic havoc we are planning. I would just like to say that this particular havoc takes the form of feeding mankind on one sixth of the acreage required for a carnivorous regime. The human race has no choice but to go vegetarian in the foreseeable future and it is better to go than be pushed. Change now and be prepared for the inevitable.

So what should we do? Initially no more than arouse general interest by lighting lamps on each of these many paths and letting travellers pick their own routes. For do not all these paths converge?

Make no mistake. We are winning through. Our meetings are better attended, our exhibitions are packed and we are no longer ignored by Press, Radio and Television. The walls of apathy are crumbling and through the cracks there is discernable a distinct odour of hostility. Hostility is a mile-stone on the road to success — it is recognition.

We have nothing to fear in this bloodless revolution. The opposing forces are defecting to our side in ever increasing numbers so let us charitably and with safety concede the last word to the enemy. I quote from the Meat Traders Journal . . . 'Vegetarianism is creeping through the Country like an insidious disease and affecting our returns.'

Platform Notes

The lecture is divided into seven parts which makes it a useful example for the purpose of illustrating the treatment. The platform notes could be boldly set out on one sheet but a much better arrangement would be nine postcards joined loosely by treasury tags so that they can be flicked over as dealt with. Why nine? Because the front one contains only the main title for identification if you accumulate a multiplicity of lecture notes, and the back one is blank but is folded half way down to make a rest — a very inexpensive pocket size portable lectern!

Now for the numbered section notes:

1. Thou shalt not be different. Plagued by zealots whom I thought to be mad.
    Indigestion enforced less critical listening.
    In the pursuit of other causes I met many vegetarians too many to be just coincidence.
    I become one of the mad minority.

2. Vegetarians become so for diverse reasons.
    They disagree with each other and spend too much time criticizing each other — practising intolerance within instead of combatting intolerance without.

3. Does vegetarianism mean renunciation? Not for long.
    It is a positive policy.
    Better to try it than to read about it.

4. Why is there always opposition to change?
    Because there is security in conformity.
    New ideas must overcome apathy and prejudice to prove their worth.

5. <u>Prominent Vegetarians</u>
   John Wesley
   General Booth
   G. B. Shaw
   County Leo Tolstoy
   Albert Schweitzer etc.
   <u>If they be mad I would be proud to be locked up alongside.</u>

6. <u>Ammunition</u>
   The horrors of factory farming.
   Economic necessity.

7. <u>Then what should we do?</u>
   People are interested by such diverse interests.
   We can <u>light lamps on each route</u> — <u>all lead to the same destination.</u>
   <u>Last word to the enemy</u> — quote from Meat Traders Journal.

The above notes are still lengthy but reasonable for so long an address.

   After a number of rehearsals they might be cut but avoid the risk of omitting key points in the sequence and so weakening the case.

Example 3

After Dinner Speeches
It is nearly impossible to provide a model as circumstances are infinitely variable, but some hints may be useful. The opening should be formal such as 'Mr Chairman (or 'Mr President' as may be appropriate), distinguished guests, Ladies and Gentlemen . . .'. This may be followed by 'I am very privileged to be asked to address you' or the like, but *do not overdo that approach*. Exaggerated modesty and/or praise are not convincing.
   Now we have to consider why you have been invited to give the

address. If you are a specialist in a subject of general or particular interest you have probably been invited for that reason and something fairly serious on your own subject is clearly indicated, but even so it should not be too serious or too long. Many guests will be present for purely social reasons so do include some interesting or amusing anecdotes if possible, and if the subject is a grim one do not labour it and spoil a convivial dinner — it will be counter-productive however worthy the cause. Otherwise keep to the guidance given for lectures.

Should your allotted task be no more than being asked to 'say a few words' before proposing the toast, then just try to be brief and preferably amusing. Do not make a lecture of it. One or two snappy funny stories will go down better than a wealth of wisdom. I would, however, suggest testing your stories on a few friends first as they may be new jokes to you but better known than you had thought. This is a very common mistake. True stories of personal incidents can be much more entertaining than 'chestnuts'. A further warning is desirable. If you do not have the gift of raising a laugh it is useless to attempt it. The outcome is usually rather pathetic.

The sort of ending I like would go something like this: 'Having halted the flow of happy conversation for too long already, I will now, to your relief, resume my seat, and I thank you for listening so patiently.'

Before we come to an analysis of meeting procedures which can make or mar the whole event a brief warning is appropriate as it can even be a speaker's opening remarks which invite failure.

Do not at any time criticize the premises where you are speaking or any of the comforts provided. Such a warning may seem to you superfluous so let me tell you how an entire lecture that had taken much organizing was thrown away in the first half minute.

I arranged for an eminent speaker to address an association of which I was a committee member. The room in question was the biggest and best in a large building, panelled and imposing, and the strings pulled to secure this particular room in honour of that speaker were many. Although this happened thirty-five years ago I can still hear his opening words as he said 'In spite of this gloomy room I will try to give you a cheerful address.' There followed a deathly hush and he might just as well have gone home for he had alienated every member present, me included. He was speaking in the holy of holies — for the first and last time.

5. Chairmanship and Meeting Procedure

Of the many books of reference on procedure at meetings and on the conduct of the Chair none is comprehensive nor ever can be for the simple reason that any organization is free to make its own rules within the bounds of Common Law. Nevertheless in essentials a fairly general pattern has evolved.

Familiarity with this framework is desirable for those who serve on committees or otherwise assist at societies' functions. For those who may be called upon to take the chair such knowledge should be regarded as essential. More dissension arises out of points of order than out of the subject matter under discussion so it is hardly surprising that good chairmen are rarer than good speakers.

The advantages of natural aptitude and of experience cannot be denied but you really do not know your potential until you have tried. It *must* help to know what you are trying to do and if the ensuing chapters get you off to a good start the rest will come in time and, who knows, you may wind up on the Woolsack.

i. The Convenor
Following a decision by a group of persons, usually a committee, to hold a meeting for any purpose it is necessary to depute somebody to convene, that is call together, such a meeting. Such a person is dubbed 'Convenor' and will be responsible for taking the necessary action to get the project launched. In more cases than not the secretary of the organization concerned will assume such responsibility as a

matter of course but with minor meetings such as subcommittees it may be one of those concerned with the specific project. If this seems a trifle obvious I can only say it can be disastrous to take it for granted and find out later that each person concerned assumed it had been taken care of, only to find out later that nothing had been done at all.

There are of course standing arrangements for regular meetings but even then it had had to be established initially who was responsible for a change in the arrangements at any time might be inadequately circulated.

For public meetings the matter of advertising the event may or may not fall upon the appointed convenor and this must be clarified at the start as must the question of engaging and/or communicating with the speaker on matters of time and place. All this is reasonably obvious but in convening a business meeting many other factors come in and some reference to the rules of the organization is essential. A convenor must know who is entitled to be notified, how long a notice is required and by what date and to whom all advance notices of motion or nominations for election need to be sent. At a certain later date before the meeting it will probably be obligatory to send out copies of the agenda to all who may be so entitled.

It is expected that the convenor will not only attend the meeting but will arrive early to see that all is ready. Some caretakers set out the room as will be needed — others do not, especially if they have not been properly informed of requirements.

There should be adequate seating and a platform table with not fewer than three chairs, and provision should be made in advance for special needs such as a blackboard or easel or separate tables for display, books for sale, etc.

For large meetings a thoughtful convenor will have enlisted a number of stewards to assist in the preparations, though it is not unusual for auxiliary helpers to have been appointed in advance by the committee. This particularly applies where refreshments are to be provided. It will have been laid down by the committee what refreshments shall be available, if free or to be paid for, payment a la carte, or by special tickets sold at the door.

Any charge for admission will be payable at the door so a table by the door will be another must for convenor or appointed steward. The overall responsibility for cash transactions will be with the treasurer.

All officials and helpers should be properly informed of the time-table, especially the chairman, or lots of cold tea will be served. Last minute volunteers can cause chaos moving furniture when the earlier arrivals are taking their seats. As a speaker I have had to help arrange chairs myself on several occasions. This should not happen. Once the chairman has taken his seat he is in charge, and the convenor's duties as such are over except for being available if need be to account for any lapses in the pre-meeting duties. He remains present as an ordinary member with no special authority until the closure when he will see that the society's property is removed and the room left in good order. A special case arises if the chairman has failed to turn up. It will be incumbent upon the committee members present to appoint a deputy chairman, if not pre-arranged, to open the proceedings. Only in the total absence of any members of committee is further action required of a convenor. He could call upon those present to elect a chairman (and they would probably ask him to step in) but it should be remembered that *it is a complete mistake for a convenor to assume that he is automatically in charge of any meeting*. This is a very common error, especially on subcommittees.

ii. The Secretary
This is the post that is hardest to fill in any organization as it can entail a high degree of responsibility and considerable effort. All the general correspondence will fall to the lot of the Secretary much being on his own initiative in addition to instructions from his Committee or Directors.

Whether or not the Secretary is also the Convenor it will almost certainly be his duty to prepare the Agenda for all business meetings. The format is of some importance and should open with apologies for absence (if any) from members, followed by 'Minutes of the Last Meeting'. These should be read out unless previously circulated to members, in which case the chairman may rule that they be 'taken as read'. Members may make objections to items which they believe to be wrongly recorded, and must be corrected if it is agreed that error has arisen. When the meeting is satisfied, the minutes should be signed by the chairman and become a part of the official records of the organization.

The next item will be 'Matters Arising from the Minutes'. Members will raise queries, e.g. on whether suggestions in the minutes have been suitably followed up, and the appropriate member will be asked to report, but this will not apply if there is a special item on the subject further down in the agenda, and the chairman will so direct.

The above items apply at any business meeting. If it be a committee meeting the minutes will be those of the last committee meeting. If it is an Annual General Meeting the minutes read will be those of the previous Annual General Meeting. In committee proceedings the agenda would continue with progress reports from members or subcommittees and new suggestions submitted.

The Secretary is usually called upon to read out any relevant correspondence before or during this phase of the meeting.

The Treasurer's report on financial matters can be listed before or after other reports as may be convenient.

The penultimate item should be 'Any Other Business' allowing for anything to be discussed not specifically listed.

Lastly, always include 'Date and Place of Next Meeting'. A great deal of unnecessary writing and telephoning follows if this is not done. Now if the meeting be an Annual General Meeting it must include, after the minutes and matters arising, the secretary's (or committee's) annual report, followed by the treasurers accounts and report.

This is usually followed by 'Election of Officers' and for this item the rules should be studied as each society has its own regulations for nominating, electing or re-electing officers including the auditor. The appointment of auditor should *not* be arranged by the treasurer.

In the larger societies nominations are submitted by the membership who have been circularized in advance and postal ballots for the actual election are increasingly done by the members in advance, and only results are announced at the Annual General Meeting.

The above is mainly for the guidance of the secretary, but is nevertheless of general interest to all concerned, as are other notes on appointments and on voting methods appearing in the sections on Miscellaneous Matters and Chairman's Duties which should be read in conjunction with this section.

At a public meeting the secretarial duties are comparatively light. Effecting introductions, taking notes if required and making announcements about covers it except perhaps for arranging for the distribution or display of literature and coping with general enquiries in the interval, if any, and before and after the proceedings.

It is at a business meeting that the secretary is the hardest worked and least applauded. In addition to any of the above functions which may be applicable he is required to sit by the chairman throughout and to be a substantial prop. Usually there is some continuity in office as compared with chairmanship which may be subject to frequent changes and may even be a once only appointment for the occasion. It is therefore expected that:

The secretary will be in possession of past minutes, membership lists, rules and regulations, and will be ready to advise the chairman on request of all recorded facts related to the agenda under discussion. If he is a paid official he may give an opinion if so invited but if he is a member holding honorary rank he will be as free as any other member to contribute.

A good secretary will be more than an informant, he will be a prompter (lots of tact needed here!) and will advise the chairman when he has reason to believe that a motion is contrary to the rules or that discussion is ensuing based on false premises of which, by reason of his office, he has better or more recent knowledge.

To take down the minutes and absorb their implications is no small task but not quite so bad as it might at first appear. The minutes are not a 'Hansard' verbatim report. Usually only the actual motions are recorded, not the interim discussions, just the result. Motions and resolutions will be covered in a later chapter. The chairman may direct other items to be minuted but the basic requirements are fairly standard and the rest will depend on custom and specific direction.

iii. The Treasurer

Most associations separate the financial duties from the secretarial. The post of treasurer is most advantageously undertaken by some one with at least elementary accounts experience, but this is not essential except for a big organization with multiple interests.

Any methodical person can do the job which basically entails collecting subscriptions and donations, keeping records thereof, and of all outward payments made. It should be emphasized that the treasurer is expected to settle liabilities as approved by the committee and is not normally free to incur or defray liabilities on his own initiative.

Similarly a treasurer can be called upon to give the benefit of his experience in financial deliberations, but the appointment does not carry the authority to direct the finances of the body he is elected to serve. A treasurer may find himself busily engaged at public meetings as he will be responsible for all cash received from admittance charges, refreshments, book sales, and possibly donations and subscriptions. Appropriate forms and receipts should be at the ready. If the event is a bazaar or jumble sale he will need a strong briefcase and plenty of small change.

It is almost superfluous to say that a treasurer will be expected by the auditor to produce, in due course, supporting vouchers for outgoings wherever reasonably obtainable. Expenses defrayed on behalf of himself or other members should be detailed and receipted and he should be aware of any rules or standing orders as to limitations on such claims.

Most societies have bank accounts and empower the treasurer to sign cheques, but they generally arrange that cheques shall all be signed by at least one other person so deputed. To cover a treasurer's unavoidable absence by reason of prolonged sickness, holiday, etc., it is advisable to have agreed emergency arrangements such as the chairman and one other named person to be allowed to act. The bank will need to have a record of all valid signatures.

The whole committee will usually have plenty to say on finance generally and on many and various ways of raising funds, but a treasurer can also be a 'treasure', as they call a good servant, if he weighs in with suggestions in this field and helps to give effect thereto. We all know about raffles, jumble sales and heart-rending charity appeals, but original ideas should always be considered, especially from the member in the key position to know the extent of the cash needed for the enterprise and the availability thereof.

Note that there are many press adverts offering fund raising novelties. Some may be good!

There arc adequate books on all branches of accountancy without my intrusion into this field within the scope of this volume, but it might be appropriate to give some brief advice to any one taking on a treasurership on the strength of some office experience and who may not be aware of the essential differences between the accounts of trading and non-trading concerns.

The day to day records may need only a columnar cash book, a ledger often proving to be unnecessary. The end of year accounts for presentation to the society's auditors and subsequently to the Annual General Meeting for the approval of members is quite another matter. It is as well to study previous years' accounts of the same organization as a guide as to what is, to them, acceptable, but a study of the final accounts of other bodies may prove very useful too. Some variety of presentation will be revealed and you will need to understand the diverse reasons for the differences should you feel tempted to change the format for your society. This applies especially if you are serving a charity. A registered charity enjoys the benefit of Income

Tax exemption but is bound by fairly tight rules.

All charities and most other societies are non-profit making, any excess of income over expenditure being subsequently applied for the benefit of the cause for which they stand, and certainly not by way of dividends in cash or kind to the members.

This brings us to the format of the final Accounts. Where there is no 'Profit' as such you cannot have a 'Profit and Loss Account'. The choice open to you is between:

(a) Receipts and Payments Account
(b) Income and Expenditure Account

You should in either case have also a Balance Sheet, of which more anon.

A 'Receipts and Payments Account' is simply a summary of the final totals in your cash book, showing cash in hand at start and finish and all the intermediate payments in and out. This method is out of date and not to be recommended as it does not reveal the true position. Cash passing during the year may relate wholly or partly to debts incurred in respect of the years before or after the date lines.

The alternative is an 'Income and Expenditure Account' which shows in the year's account only the amounts applicable to that year. To get a true picture one must even split a single item, as for example a membership subscription paid for more than one year or a room rental paid for a period in arrears or in advance. This form of account simplifies the preparation of a Balance Sheet showing all the liabilities and assets at the final date.

What must above all be avoided is a mixture of methods (a) and (b) above, either in fact or in only the choice of words used in the heading. By this is meant, for example, a 'Receipts and Expenditure Account' or an 'Income and Payments Account', both of which are entirely meaningless. If you think it would not arise I assure you it can and it does. 'Income and Payments Account' was the actual heading of the annual accounts of a large Society to which I belonged.

In this particular case the error was only in the title. It correctly presented the accounts in the form of an income and expenditure acount, but how the auditors came to pass them under a wrong and misleading heading I shall never know.

These observations are not made to dissuade any one from accepting such office but rather to indicate that it may be wise to seek a little guidance at the outset from the retiring treasurer or from the auditor rather than just before having to present the accounts for the year. Some societies delight in making their final accounts for the year incomprehensible. Do not lose sight of the real object of the exercise which is to show members how their Society stands. They want to know the rival merits of the various sources of income and just what it was spent on. Is there a shortage of funds necessitating economies or bigger contributions?, or is there a surplus and a venturesome policy could be justified? Most modern income and expenditure accounts show last year's figures in brackets or in a separate column for comparison. This is sound and to be encouraged.

Try to keep it simple. Your members are not all accountants and you are doing it for them.

Income used to be listed on the left and expenditure on the right. Currently it is more usual to arrange the lists vertically and treat the balance sheet similarly. The example following shows the accounts in their simplest forms and you will note that all amounts are shown in pounds only. Having once balanced your accounts you enter your several items to the nearest pound, and if it is then a pound or two out in the final totals it will be because a number of items ending in, say, 35p or thereabouts have been written down to even pounds. It will readily be appreciated that one or more items may have to be written up or down by a pound to effect a balance. No one will mind this and the simpler presentation will be appreciated by your members.

Example of the Annual set of Accounts for a Society — *entirely ficitious*:

The South London Lecture and Debating Society
INCOME and EXPENDITURE ACCOUNT
for the Year ended 31 March, 1982

Income	1982	1981
Members' Subscriptions	116	94
Donations	5	—
Interest — Bank Deposit Account	10	6
Surplus on Summer Garden Party	12	9
Annual Dinner	9	12
Coach Outing	4	—
Christmas Social	7	5
Sales of Literature	18	14
Sales of Refreshments	12	11
Expenditure	£193	£151
Lecturers' Fees and Expenses	29	21
Postage and Telephone	27	19
Printing and Stationery	18	15
Typing and Duplicating	14	12
Hire of Halls	24	18
Bank Charges	5	4
Sundry Expenses	9	7
	£126	£96
Excess of Income over Expenditure Transferred to General Fund	£67	£55

BALANCE SHEET 31 March, 1982

General Fund	1982	1981
Balance at 31 March, 1981	147	92
Add Excess of Income over Expenditure for the year ended 31 March, 1982	67	55
	£214	£147

Represented By:

Current Assets
Balance at Bank: Barclays Bank Ltd.

	1982	1981
Deposit Account	120	80
Current Account	54	43
Cash in Hand	13	8
Sundry Debtors	20	10
Stock of Literature	15	12
	£222	£153

William Willing
Hon. Treasurer

(The Auditor will in due course add a statement such as the following
and it will appear on the printed copies for distribution.)

*I have examined the books and vouchers of the South London Lecture
and Debating Society and certify that the Income and Expenditure Account
gives a correct record of the Society's transactions for the year ended
31 March, 1982 and that the Balance Sheet is a true statement of the
financial position of the Society at that date.*

A. I. Checker,
Honorary Auditor.

iv. Committee Meetings

These meetings are less formal than general or public meetings but
nevertheless need to be taken quite seriously as the very life of the
organization depends on their plans and preparations.

Although it is customary for members to remain seated, usually
round a table, they are governed by a Chairman who may be appointed
on a continuous basis at the Annual General Meeting or may be elected
by the committee members themselves according to the rules of the
society.

The secretary is normally the convenor and even if the meetings
are in a fixed place at prescribed regular times he should send notices
to all committee members, with the agenda, for each occasion. As
he will be responsible for reading the minutes of the last meeting at
each ensuing one he may streamline the proceedings by circulating
copies thereof in advance. Much time may be saved at the meeting.
In the absence of any objections minutes are often 'taken as read' on
a show of hands and signed as correct by the Chairman.

The following item on the Agenda should be 'Matters arising from
the Minutes' and these will be well-considered items if members have
had the benefit of prior perusal.

It is usual for the secretary to take the minutes at any meeting. These
must include all motions, resolutions and anything else the chairman
specifically directs to be recorded. It is not necessary to take down

discussions but should name proposers and seconders of Motions and the results of the voting thereon which could be, for example, 'Four votes for the motion and two against. The motion was therefore declared carried'.

When all are in favour one may record 'carried unanimously' but be very careful to make sure that no eligible voter has abstained. In such a case although the remainder be of one opinion it is not unanimous and must be recorded as 'nem con'. There is a significant difference (see also page 78).

All correspondence to and from the society should be available for reference at committee meetings and may be required to be read out under appropriate items on the agenda.

The penultimate item on any Agenda should be 'Any Other Business' and the last should be 'Date, Time and Place of Next Meeting' (frequently forgotten!, see also page 64).

It cannot be over-emphasized that decisions taken at a committee or subcommittee meeting are quite useless if no one is deputed to act thereon. Members who sit 'in an advisory capacity' are not as a rule much help and tend to lengthen meetings and overload the 'willing horses'. If this seems to be the trend a committee chairman can get results by announcing that no further suggestions will be accepted unless accompanied by an offer. It really works!

For a major project the committee would probably appoint a sub-committee to act, or if necessary to investigate, and report back. For simpler matters it is usual to enlist one or more volunteers.

v. Subcommittees

It is undesirable for full committees to enter into long and detailed discussions on every item on the agenda. Long sittings may be avoided and much more achieved by the appointment of a small subcommittee of a few members only to investigate fully a certain matter and report their findings to the main committee at the next meeting.

Normally a few suitable persons are elected from those present by reason of their special knowledge or ability relating to the matter in question but other names may be suggested and absent members may be nominated and will be included subject to acceptance when asked. It should be noted that membership of a subcommittee does not qualify any one to attend meetings of the main committee except by special invitation.

Just as committees have the right to co-opt members to fill gaps caused by resignations or sickness, so may a sub-committee co-opt. The rules may require a subcommittee to get approval first. It may even be permissible within the rules of the society for a subcommittee to co-opt a non-member of the society by reason of having special knowledge on a particular subject involved. This would, however, be on a short term basis with no voting rights. It would probably be better to invite such a person as a consultant and not as a committee member at all.

Some subcommittees may be, and frequently are, Standing Subcommittees, as, for example, a Catering Subcommittee which would be responsible for the refreshments at all appropriate functions. Such a subcommittee would need formal re-appointment annually by the Main Committee.

The secretary of the society frequently, but not necessarily, serves on a subcommittee but it is not his duty to arrange their meetings and prepare agenda thereof unless so instructed. On the appointment of any subcommittee a convenor is appointed from their number who will call meetings by arrangement with the others.

It is important to note that the convenor is *not* automatically appointed chairman of the subcommittee. He should open the proceedings by asking his fellow members if they wish to elect a chairman for the meeting. They may well ask him to take the chair, which he may agree to do, but a very small group need not have a chairman at all. It is, however, necessary in any large subcommittee if business is to be conducted efficiently.

In a standing subcommittee the members may elect a chairman on a continuous basis but the main committee is entitled to ignore the status and look to the appointed convenor to present reports. This has happened to me. In my case I was both convenor and, by unanimous consent, chairman of a large subcommittee on a continuous basis subject only to confirmation at intervals. Nevertheless the main committee took exception to my reports being signed as 'Chairman', and although I got away with it for quite a long time I feel bound to record that it is not technically correct and I would not advise others to try it on.

One more point. A subcommittee is not *required* to take minutes but may do so and I do recommend this course. As with principal committees the minutes are signed by the chairman at the following meeting when they are read out and passed as correct (or as corrected!). It was my custom to submit the subcommittee minutes by way of a report. This proved acceptable and that is exactly how I got away with it, neatly bending the rules for five years or more.

vi. The Chairman

i. *Getting started*
The Chairman is in control of the meeting. Any and every meeting. Even if it is only a subcommittee meeting if as many as five are present it should be remembered that small boats also need rudders and the business in hand will take a smoother course and reach its destination much quicker with a curb on drifting.

It is clearly desirable that chairmen should be conversant not only with normal meeting procedure but with the rules governing the particular event he is chairing. While he is fully entitled to lean heavily on the secretary in respect of the rules of the association holding the meeting, his conduct of the proceedings will fall very far short of requirements if he is not versed in the basic principles and customs. The secretary on request may quote the rules or provide information but decisions on procedure and on the interpretation of a rule rest with the chairman whose ruling is final.

These remarks apply to any meeting but more particularly to the business type of event which of necessity dominates this section of the book.

ii. Carrying on

Motions

Usually any member may propose a motion but it cannot be debated or voted on unless it has a seconder with the exception of motions from the chair which need no seconder. Priority should be given to written motions sent in in advance and appearing on the agenda together with names of proposer and seconder. All motions, written or verbal should be clearly read out by the chairman or by the secretary if so directed. It is then the proposer's privilege to 'Speak to the Motion' and the seconder may follow immediately or reserve the right to speak later after some discussion has ensued. Speeches in opposition should be given just as much time as the supporters' contributions but to avoid unduly lengthy discussion and repetition the chairman is in order to request brevity and may see fit to impose time limits. He should of course endeavour to be scrupulously fair between the rival factions, especially when closing the discussion to take a vote and exercising his privilege to sum up if he thinks there is any confusion.

It is open to other members, who feel that the discussion has gone on long enough, to take action. A member may move that 'The motion be now put'. The chairman must ask if there is a seconder and providing there is then he must ask for a show of hands. A majority vote on this point obliges the chairman to put the motion to the vote without further debate but before allowing this to arise he should be sure the principals had had their say and draw attention for instance to a seconder not having been given his reserved rights.

Once a motion has been voted on and passed by a requisite majority it becomes a *Resolution* which is binding and cannot be amended so we must next deal with amendments before we go on to methods of voting.

Amendments

Any motion can be stopped before the vote is taken by a member proposing an amendment, which must be duly seconded, and a discussion will usually ensue followed by a vote on the amendment. If it be passed then the motion should be read out with the amendment incorporated and voted on in that form. Would that that were the whole story but life is not that simple. As often as not there will be other amendments, each separately debated and then incorporated or rejected as the voting may require. But worse is to come. There can be an amendment to an amendment before the original amendment is voted on and the last must be settled first and work back in that order. It can be very difficult to keep track and the final vote must be on the original Motion as amended.

The chairmain has to watch for amendments that are really alternative motions. They must not be accepted as amendments though the substance thereof may well enter into the discussions and those who prefer an alternative proposal should endeavour to gain their end by voting against the motion (amended or otherwise) and, if it be rejected, introduce the new motion.

Two more points remain on amendments. One is that there is no objection to the apparent contradiction of voting *for* an amendment when you are opposed to the whole motion because you may very well feel that second best to throwing out a motion you find unacceptable may be suffering only a less unacceptable amended version. It is a precautionary measure prior to trying to get all your own way.

The other point is that the proposer of a motion who senses that the members are against him may elect to save further trouble and perhaps acrimonious discussion by simply asking leave to withdraw the motion. This can be permitted at the chairman's discretion subject only to the assent of the seconder and may be wholly disallowed if the members feel that it should be put to the vote for any reason at all. One reason might be that supporters felt the proposer had 'cold feet' and could have gone on to win, and another might be that a clear majority vote against the motion might insure against it being brought up again at the first convenient occasion. Once in the minutes as a rejected motion it would not be permitted on the agenda again unless the circumstances had altered.

Once a resolution has been recorded it will require to be acted upon and the chairman should ascertain who is willing and able to act upon the decisions taken. This may appropriately fall upon the secretary, but it could be necessary to place the responsibility in the hands of a sub-committee, either existing or to be set up for the purpose. Any such arrangement should be minuted.

Voting
This is not as simple as might be supposed. It can be quite simple, especially at a small meeting, but it is necessary to know the variations.

It is usual to take a show of hands in the first place and if it is overwhelmingly one way it is acceptable. Any doubt should be removed by a count and perhaps a recount if close but there are circumstances in which a show of hands is inadequate. All present may not have the right to vote and an unauthorised vote could not be easily detected this way. On an important issue or a close vote it is safer to have voting papers distributed to those to whom it applies and to appoint tellers to collect and count the votes. They should report their figures to the chairman who will announce the outcome. It is very important to record a correct verdict and fatally easy to fall into the trap of announcing the passing or rejecting of a motion as being unanimous when all the votes go one way. There may be *abstainers* in which case the verdict is 'nem con' which means 'none against' and this is not the same thing at all. An abstainer may raise a protest if his deliberate abstention is ignored.

There is yet another kind of voting to consider before we pass on, and that is a Poll. Voting rights may vary, especially at a meeting of delegates from branches of an organization. Delegates may be entitled by the rules to vote in accordance with the numbers of members they represent and if so this needs to be shown on the voting papers and the grand total of all votes will decide the issue.

There is often controversy on the matter of the customary right of a chairman to settle an equal vote by exercising his right to record a *casting vote*. This is open to more than one meaning and a chairman should make quite sure he knows his rights before applying them. He may be entitled to vote *only* when there is a tie or he may have a normal vote as a member with an additional vote to employ when the figures equal out. The rules should be clear on this but unfortunately are not always so and a wise chairman would not use two votes unless specifically so entitled. There is, however, no obligation to use the casting vote at all and unless the issue has to be settled one way or the other as a matter of urgency the wiser course is usually not to use the privilege. An equal vote means a strong division of opinion which may resolve itself in time and cause less dissension when members have had more time to think about it and the stronger views have cooled off a bit. A 'dead heat' automatically carries the item forward to the next meeting and often achieves this end.

There remains only the matter of passing motions without taking a vote. (This is not a misprint — I do mean '*no vote*'.) A chairman should at all times sense the feeling of the meeting and on minor issues on which it is perfectly clear that there is complete unison it is entirely superfluous to waste time counting. A chairman would in such circumstances say something like 'We seem to be of one mind. Shall I take it that you wish me to record this motion as passed (or rejected)?' General cries of assent will be deemed sufficient for the secretary to record the passage of the motion in the minutes. Any member may of course insist on a vote being taken.

iii. And when Others 'carry on'

Points of Order

At any meeting and at any time a member may stand up and say 'Mr Chairman, on a point of order' and the chairman is under an obligation to take his point as a matter of priority.

It is hardly surprising that this rule is open to convenient misunderstanding by those who wish to interrupt in their own interests so it must be fully understood by all chairmen. A point of order means exactly what it says and concerns procedure and *not* the subject matter.

A permissible point of order might be that the person speaking at the time the member stood up to make his point was in fact, for some reason within the rules, not entitled to speak at all. Another reason might be that the meeting had a time limit which had been exceeded. Whatever it may be it must concern the conduct of the meeting and not be used to get in an opinion on the debate.

Chairmen be warned. You will be lucky indeed if no one ever tries it on and the most usual and sometimes very subtle way of doing it is to challenge a statement by the person speaking. For example, 'On a point of order, Mr Chairman, the population of this country is not a hundred million, it is only about half that figure.' That was not a point of order at all. It was point of *fact* and entirely out of order. Watch it! A persistent offender should be openly reprimanded and disallowed further participation in the discussions. A genuine point of procedure raised at the right time may, on the other hand, save a lengthy discussion on something outside the scope of the meeting which the chairman had inadvertently allowed to be brought up. One wide-awake member might remember that the topic under discussion had already been left to a subcommittee to investigate and further mention pending their report was out of order and time-wasting.

Interruptions
Subtle pseudo-points of order are by no means the only unauthorised punctuations to the procedure. There are variations on the theme from calling out a quick word or two to shouting a speaker down, and others may join in and make a Babel of it. Tolerating offenders is not a noble act of leniency — it is surrender to a noisy minority at the expense of all else present. The majority will be solidly behind you if you find yourself in one of these uncomfortable chairs (not called 'the hot seat' without reason) and you assert your authority and refuse to let the meeting continue until interrupters have subsided. Probably the most difficult task of all is to be firm with offenders well-known to you and senior to you, perhaps, but have no fear. I have never heard a chairman criticized for being strong whereas sloppy

chairmen are seldom invited to fulfil the role again. Keep your temper, be firm but not rude and the first interruption of the meeting will probably be the last.

Heckling
This must have some brief separate mention because there is a very big difference between trying to get a point of view in out of turn and trying to wreck a meeting. Some hecklers do not actually say anything but just shout or otherwise make a noise by way of protest. This is more or less limited to political meetings with highly controversial issues under discussion and need not be anticipated at the sewing circle's monthly meeting or whatever.

Ejection should be a last resort and the mere threat of it will silence all but the brave. Do not even threaten it if you have no one there able and willing to carry it out if need be.

When any meeting becomes overheated and tempers are rising a very good way to get calm is to adjourn rather than close down. Call a break for ten minutes and some of the mutual valedictions may get ironed out over a cup of tea or a stroll down the corridor. Chapter One of this book drew attention to the value and power of silence. It is really a potent force.

Emergencies
Talking of maintaining calm, in the event of fire, accident, or any other unpredictable possible cause of panic the chairman is captain of the ship and should keep his position on the bridge and endeavour to direct, a display of calm from the chair being more likely to mitigate the trouble than anything else.

At all times while a meeting is in session the chair should not be vacated and a chairman who is obliged to leave the platform (to take an urgent telephone call for example) should put someone else in that seat until he gets back. There is always somebody in charge on the bridge.

The Quorum

Having clarified the functions of those officiating in their several capacities we can now take it from the point where the convenor passes authority to the chair. It may be appropriate for the chairman to say a few words of welcome to the assembly before proceeding with the agenda which will have been placed before him and with which he will already be familiar unless he has been asked to deputise at short notice. *But wait!* Before starting any business he has to know whether according to the rules the meeting even exists — which brings us to the important question of the *Quorum*.

The quorum is the minimum number of members present to make the meeting valid and decisions binding. This is a very necessary rule without which an unrepresentative minority could rush through resolutions quite unacceptable to many who were not able to attend or arrived too late to stop 'a fast one' being pulled. The quorum should and usually does vary with the nature of the meeting. A committee would obviously have a smaller minimum than a general meeting but perhaps not quite so obvious is the distinction customarily applied to major changes such as dissolution of the organization. The rules will usually require two-thirds or even three-quarters of those present to pass such a change and the quorum could be a very high figure as compared with ordinary general meetings. A check is advisable.

It had not been my intention to elaborate any further on this matter but a situation arose at an Annual General Meeting at which I was present recently. The meeting looked unlikely to get started as we were waiting for a number of expected but still absent members after quite a long time. We were short of a quorum and the chairman felt obliged to do nothing except wait, hope, and if necessary adjourn until further notice. I took it upon myself to make a suggestion which the chairman put to those present and the meeting proceeded by common consent on the understanding that no resolutions could be passed until a quorum was present and the late arrivals be asked to ratify any minor decisions taken in the interim. This enabled half an hour of useful work to be covered with no breach of the rules as far as I could see. There were certainly no dissenters in this case but had objections been voiced or any of the agenda involved been controversial, the proceedings would have been stopped at once and deferred as necessary.

It rather depends on the precise rules of the association concerned. The safest course for a chairman in any doubt or faced by a voiced objection is to refrain from conducting any business in the absence of a quorum for any part of the proceedings.

Rules should include a time limit for awaiting late arrivals before taking the appropriate action, but in the absence thereof the chairman must exercise his discretion.

One last point before we drop the question of Quorums. If members leave the meeting temporarily or finally before any motion is resolved the same rule must apply. Those remaining cannot make valid decisions if they are too few to form a quorum but their departure will not invalidate the whole meeting. Previous decisions taken will stand.

Subject then to the requisite number being present the chairman may proceed with the agenda. It should be noted that he is not bound to take it in the order as laid out. It has probably been arranged in a logical sequence, dictated to some extent by custom, but he does have discretionary powers which it may well be expedient to use. Certain members will have proposed motions in advance and both proposer and seconder should be present to speak. It would be very wrong to take such a motion in their absence and the agenda should be rearranged to suit circumstances including, when possible, considering a motion earlier than listed when those affected have to leave for valid reasons before time. There may of course be standing orders laid down to cover these points. As well to check.

vii. Miscellaneous Matters

i. Elections and Appointments
In almost every democratically constituted association the paid staff,

if any, are appointed by the committee and are not subject to election by the members generally. All honorary officers are normally elected at each Annual General Meeting and it is only by reference to the rules that one may hope to know just what officers the association has, how many may be elected to the committee and whether or not there are restrictions on the number of years any one person may serve consecutively.

In the absence of additional nominations it is in order for a committee to be re-elected *en bloc* but if the number nominated exceeds the permissible total as limited by the rules, then voting is required. It should be specially mentioned that rules vary on the mode of election of the chairman of the committee. The more usual is for the committee themselves at their first committee meeting following the Annual General Meeting to elect their chairman, but some societies require that the chairman be selected by the members generally. The committee members are usually in a better position to judge which of their number is most capable. No member should ever be elected to any position in his absence except provisionally and subject to later assent.

Subject to limits and restrictions in the rules it is customary for committees to be free to co-opt members to fill a vacancy arising from a resignation but such office is temporary and does not survive an election. If the co-opted member does not get elected to the committee at the next Annual General Meeting and his or her services are still required then the member must be formally reco-opted, if still required.

Another reason for enlisting extra members to a committee is to get help on particular projects. In such cases the co-option should terminate with the end of the special business and attendance at meetings may reasonably be limited to the actual time the particular subject is under review. *Consultants* called in who are not members of the society should definitely attend only for the particular subject. It should be checked whether co-opted members have any voting rights.

ii. Annual General Meetings

This has been fully covered under Secretaries' and Chairman's duties, but a warning note about 'The Annual Report to Members' is appropriate.

This document is usually a recital of the year's activities and is read out at the Annual General Meeting whether previously circulated or not and is then briefly discussed and approved by the members. There would not seem to be much to say about this and I might have refrained had I not witnessed something very near to a fight on the platform on one memorable occasion.

The question is whose report is it? The correct answer is that it is the committee's report to the members and not the secretary's. The secretary may, and often does, prepare an initial draft, but it needs the committee's approval and as many amendments as they may see fit to introduce before it is passed for the chairman of the committee to sign.

iii. Extra-Ordinary General Meetings

This title covers any business meeting other than the Annual General. All members must be notified in adequate time, as laid down in the rules of the association, and it should be noted that the quorum may be different from that specified for the Annual General Meeting (see sub-heading 'The Quorum' and 'The Chairman').

Such meetings are called for urgent matters that cannot await the next Annual General Meeting, as for example, amalgamation with another association, the replacement of a senior official, a necessary immediate change in the rules, or even the dissolution of the association.

The agenda must include nothing but the urgent matter for which the meeting had been called, and no other subject may be introduced before or during the meeting.

iv. Lecture Meetings

The conduct of public meetings has been largely covered but mainly from the speaker's point of view. Viewing it more from the chair it is much less exacting than the business meeting but nevertheless a chairman can make or mar the occasion. He must watch the time and take some steps to curb loquacious speakers (pointing to the clock will usually have the desired effect, but some speakers ask to receive a signal when time is running out).

It is the chairman's responsibility and not the speaker's to see that those who wish to raise questions are taken in order, are not allowed a second question while others are waiting, and that comments other than questions are taken separately and later if time permits. Time should always be left for the speaker to sum up.

After the chairman has declared the meeting closed the platform should be vacated and further attempts at questions totally ignored. If the chairman does not run the meeting the meeting will run the chairman.

v. Discussions and Debates

It is customary to arrange for one person to be nominated to lead a discussion and although he will give mainly his own view he is not a good leader if he is too conclusive. It should be made clear that there are many viewpoints so as to encourage lively participation which then follows under the control of the chairman who should see that as many as possible have a chance to speak and he can also help by filling in awkward silences by contributions of his own.

In a *debate*, on the other hand, the appointed proposer of the motion will normally speak first and at some length. The time limit should be pre-arranged and kept to, and then a similar period should be allowed to the opposer. If there are seconders on each side they may speak next in the same order, usually for a shorter prescribed period.

In the case of a public debate it may or may not be thrown open to general discussion according to what has been pre-arranged and publicly announced, but in any case the first two speakers each have the right to sum up and they should do so in the *reverse order* from the opening speeches. The proposer is entitled to the last word.

A vote on the issue is not necessarily taken and may be most undesirable as the supporters on one side may be quite overwhelming, simply by reason of being the 'home team'. A visiting society joining in friendly debate does not expect to be made to look ridiculous, and a wise chairman will see that there does not just happen to be time left to take a vote if such a situation exists and a vote is requested by any one present.

Debates are not generally to be recommended for propaganda purposes as they tend to confuse rather than elucidate.

Other minor meetings which may perhaps be briefly mentioned are Brains Trusts in which the audience is limited to questions and the Panel supply all the answers. They do not all have to answer all the questions but may be called upon by the chairman according to their special knowledge. Two or more of the panel may of course be called upon. Quizzes are quite easy to run and open to a variety of treatments. All I would like to say on this, having run several myself, is that organizers may expect to take up to three months compiling the questions and answers and still get challenged. Be a hundred per cent certain of your answers or you need to know the rules of debates coupled with some elementary knowledge of quelling riots.

vi. Declared interests

At any business meeting a proposal may be made which could bring personal profit to the proposer or to another member of the association.

Providing the motion is genuinely in the common interest this is not in itself an offence but on the other hand there is a very definite obligation for the potential beneficiary to declare his interest. Furthermore it would be desirable for him not to vote on the issue.

Any ill-feeling can be avoided by the simple expedient of the member concerned offering to pass on to the association the proceeds of any personal gain. N.B. In the case of a charitable organization members are forbidden personal benefits altogether. Should they arise they *must* be passed on to the charity, failing which charity status could be withdrawn with the consequent loss of tax concessions.

viii. Adjournment and Closure

At the chairman's discretion, subject to the rules or standing orders, a meeting may be adjourned to another date, specified or left open as may be desirable according to circumstances, the most usual being simply failure to cover the whole agenda in the time available. It can also be expedient to adjourn by reason of the absence of key personnel concerned with items therein which cannot advisedly be left over to the next meeting.

Another reason might be an inconclusive discussion for lack of information or sufficient consideration and it is felt that time for investigation and further thought would be helpful but it is better that the chairman, rather than bluntly state that the meeting stands adjourned, should suggest that an adjournment seems desirable and might ask if anyone would care to put such a motion. It would probably be carried and feelings all round the better for such conduct. Such cases have often arisen.

Now it is very important to note that the adjournment, when it eventually takes place, is part of the original meeting *and not a new one*. It may be convenient to read or circulate the minutes of the first part as a reminder, but there is no such obligation and it does not absolve those responsible from producing the full combined minutes at the appropriate later date. Since it is all one meeting there is no question of electing a chairman for the second session except in the unavoidable absence of the person who took the chair in the first place.

The only obligatory notices to be sent out would be to absentees from the first session. Any others need be only as directed by the chairman unless of course the date had been left open and would necessitate a general notice when settled.

Closure is not always simple. When the agenda is complete the chairman declares the meeting closed and all are free to depart. That should be simple enough but I have actually heard a *speaker* declare a meeting closed because he resented a question put to him from a member of the audience after his lecture. The chairman in this case fortunately knew his job and immediately declared the closure void and closed the meeting down himself in his own good time. It was quite a scene.

Following a lecture I gave on Meeting Procedure I had a question put to me that could hardly have been anticipated and in giving a snap reply I admitted it was tentative and that I would like time to investigate. Between then and the next meeting I consulted three experienced chairmen who all confirmed my provisional reply as being right as far as it went but between us we evolved a comprehensive answer which I now incorporate in every course I conduct. I put the question at one session and invite replies at the next because it is an exceedingly useful exercise and I am finishing this book as nearly as is possible in like manner by setting the problem and asking readers not to turn to the last page before giving quite a long time to think it out. A written answer would be best as it is so easy to say 'Ah yes, that is just what I meant to say!'

The Exercise
This is a real incident and happened, I understand, at a meeting of a Students Union.

The Union had a rule by which their regular meetings terminated at 10 p.m. unless a majority were in favour of its continuation after that hour in which case it was permissible for the meeting to continue until 10.30.

In the instance in question the meeting was somewhat heated with many members anxious to speak. At *precisely ten o'clock* the chairman stood up, declared the meeting closed and turned to leave the platform.

A member then rose to his feet and called out 'Mr Chairman, on a point of order, we are entitled to continue if a majority so wish. Will you please take a vote on it?'

The Chairman replied 'I HAVE CLOSED THE MEETING' and thereupon strode off the platform and out of the building.

The Questions
1. Should the chairman have acceded to the member's request and taken a vote?

2. If not then could the meeting have continued by any means such as by putting up a new chairman?

3. Who was in the wrong in the first place and so to cause the dilemma to arise at all?

4. How could and should the trouble have been avoided?

5. Is the rule itself at fault?

Answers overleaf.

The Answers
1.   No. The chairman, having closed the meeting, had no authority to act. There was in fact no longer a chairman and no meeting.
2.   The meeting could not continue except entirely informally with no status and no decisions taken would be binding in any way. Time would preclude convening a new immediate meeting with committee authority.
3.   The member was in the wrong to stand up and speak when he did. He was too late — see reply to Question 1. The chairman had the *right* to close the meeting at 10 p.m. in accordance with the rules and was powerless thereafter.

    But as to who was wrong in the first place the blame must be placed on both the members and the chairman who neither watched the clock and acted at the right time. Responsibility must rest mainly with the chair.
4.   Members wishing to continue could have made their point of order a few minutes before time and the chairman would be bound to take action. A vote might not be necessary if the demand for continuation were obvious. But is it not part of a chairman's duty to sense the *feeling* of a meeting? He should have asked for a show of hands some minutes before the end and in not doing so failed miserably in his duty. There is little doubt it was his last chair.
5.   As a protection against human error the rule itself might well have been framed to require a decision by, say, 9.50 but there really is no infallible method and if that earlier time were binding the same situation could still arise.

If your answers agreed reasonably well with the above then you have either had a great deal of experience or, if you are new to it all, then you must have absorbed much from the foregoing chapters and you may step with confidence into the 'Hot Seat' at any time and leave the platform unscathed afterwards.

Index

THE TOASTMASTER'S TREASURE CHEST

5,000 INDEXED ITEMS

H. V. Prochnow & H. V. Prochnow Jr. For toastmasters, businessmen, politicians — anyone likely to be called on for brief remarks — here is a storehouse of wit, wisdom, jokes, toasts, stories and quotations! An indispensable book for those involved in discussions, conferences, seminars, Rotary clubs, church groups, trade organizations. Provides you with well-prepared, stimulating, 'impromptu' remarks! *None of this duplicates the material in the Prochnows' companion volume.* **The Public Speaker's Treasure Chest** (over 500,000 copies sold).

PAINLESS PUBLIC SPEAKING

DEVELOP AND DELIVER YOUR TRAIN OF THOUGHT ANYTIME, ANYWHERE

Sharon Anthony Bower. A unique programme for practising a speech step-by-step, with techniques for overcoming stage fright, remembering your train of thought, speaking in a compelling, persuasive manner. *Includes:* Proven techniques for coping with anxiety; How to deal with difficult questions or people; Steps for organizing your train-of-thought; Light up your speech with attention-getters; Polish your speaking style; How to confront difficult personalities; How to practise the progressive relaxation exercise; Routine warm-up exercises for performers.

5,000 ONE AND TWO LINERS FOR ANY AND EVERY OCCASION

HOW TO MAKE OTHER PEOPLE LAUGH

Leopold Fechtner. A wealth of comedy material for public speakers, toast-masters, emcees, lecturers, etc. You are likely to do better in your job, make more sales, or get people to work harder for you, if you can add a bit of humour to the situation! Those who make speeches can look up appropriate gags, either under the 250 popular topics in the table of contents; or in the handy reference guide at the back which will provide a rich variety of additional or connected gags.

HUMOUR AND ELOQUENCE IN PUBLIC SPEAKING

A MASTER SPEAKER SHOWS THE EASY WAY!

Edward J. Hegarty. How to turn an ordinary speech into a dynamic, humorous and eloquent masterpiece that will get your points across quickly, easily, and memorably—while it pleases and satisfies your audience. In this book discover: 12 plans for starting any speech; 10 kinds of humour—with advice on the kinds you can use in good taste; how to find sure-fire humour material; how to tell a story; how to use figures or visuals to make your point; 16 ways to end your speech.